Children Around the World: The Ultimate Class Field Trip

Visit 14 Countries and Explore the Languages and Cultures of Children Across the Globe

Written and illustrated
by Marilee Woodfield

Publisher
Key Education Publishing Company, LLC
Minneapolis, Minnesota

CONGRATULATIONS ON YOUR PURCHASE OF A KEY EDUCATION PRODUCT!

The editors at Key Education are former teachers who bring experience, enthusiasm, and quality to each and every product. Thousands of teachers have looked to the staff at Key Education for new and innovative resources to make their work more enjoyable and rewarding. Key Education is committed to developing and publishing educational materials that will assist teachers in building a strong and developmentally appropriate curriculum for young children.

PLAN FOR GREAT TEACHING EXPERIENCES WHEN YOU USE EDUCATIONAL MATERIALS FROM KEY EDUCATION PUBLISHING COMPANY, LLC!

Credits

Author: Marilee Woodfield
Project Director: Sherrill B. Flora
Editors: Kelly Huxmann, Audrey Rose
Inside Illustrations: Marilee Woodfield
Page Design and Layout: Kelly Huxmann
Cover Design: Annette Hollister-Papp

Key Education welcomes manuscripts and product ideas from teachers. For a copy of our submission guidelines, please send a self-addressed, stamped envelope to:

**Key Education Publishing Company, LLC
Acquisitions Department
9601 Newton Avenue South
Minneapolis, Minnesota 55431**

About the Author

In addition to teaching and directing preschools for 20 years, Marilee Woodfiled graduated with a with a BS in Human Development from Brigham Young University. In addition to writing teacher resource books, Marilee spends her time teaching preschool music, driving the family taxi service and engaging in various home-improvement projects. Marilee currently resides in Texas with her husband and 4 children.

Copyright Notice

Standard Book Number: 1-933052-37-6
Children Around the World: The Ultimate Class Field Trip
Copyright © 2006 by Key Education Publishing Company, LLC
Minneapolis, Minnesota 55431

Table of Contents

Introduction

Get ready to take your students on the ultimate class field trip! Using *Children Around the World: The Ultimate Class Field Trip* as your guide, introduce children to 14 different countries, exploring the languages and cultures of children across the globe.

Teach your students how to say hello in Spanish or count to 10 in Russian. Introduce them to the foods kids eat in Italy or the games they play in Iran. Tell them tales from China and invite them to taste fresh coconut from Tahiti. These are just a few examples of the fun things you'll discover as you and your students travel the globe—right in your own classroom.

Along the way, your students will keep journals of their travels (disguised as their suitcases). And when they return, the children will be able to show off their passports—stamped with a special seal from each country they visited—and postcards of their favorite experiences in each place they visited. Students will also collect pictures of children in traditional dress as well as the flags of the countries. Help them keep updated maps of their travels so the children will be able to find their way around the globe the next time they visit their newfound friends.

Loaded with cross-curricular activities, *Children Around the World: The Ultimate Class Field Trip* integrates social awareness of the cultures and people of 14 nations around the world through reading, writing, math, large and small motor activities, science experiments, art projects, dramatic play, and cooking activities. Here are some additional tips to help make your field trip a success:

- The topics covered in this book focus primarily on mainstream cultures and traditions. Although geopolitical and religious topics are important aspects of everyday life, they have been kept to a minimum in order to keep the content current and to avoid offending someone with a careless treatment of a sacred custom. If you choose to delve more deeply into each country's experience, there are many texts and guidebooks to help you along the way.

- Use the Internet and newspapers to identify events such as war, natural disasters, and human achievements (e.g., Nobel prizes, Olympics, etc.) that are current and pertinent to each country as you learn about it.

- Before traveling the globe, take advantage of the resources right in your own backyard. Poll the parents of the children in your school. You will probably find a few who can share insights and experiences as a special visitor to your school or by loaning artifacts and other souvenirs from travels to foreign countries.

- This book includes common words, phrases, and numbers from 1 to 10 for each country explored. Do not be shy in trying out the new languages. Though you may stumble at first, the children will have fun trying to pronounce the new words with you. *(Note: Spelling of vocabulary in languages that do not use the Roman alphabet—i.e., Chinese, Hindi, Farsi, Japanese, and Russian—is phonetic and may vary from other sources. Unless otherwise noted, vocabulary has been taken from* http://www.travlang.com/languages/index.html *or from books listed in the bibliography on page 160. You can also visit the TravLang site to hear audio files of the vocabulary being spoken.)*

- A flag pattern for each country visited. Refer to the directions provided and a reference source to determine the colors of each flag. Be sure to use a variety of media when creating the flags.

- Putumayo World Music produces a variety of music from around the world. Check your local library or music stores or visit their Web site at http://www.putumayo.com.

- Embassy addresses are listed so you can obtain more information about travel to each country. You might consider having the children write to the embassies requesting information. Your students will have fun waiting for the packets to arrive in the mail, and you all just might learn something you didn't know before!

Here is a list of some of the social studies content standards addressed in this book:
- Identify rules and laws.
- Identify sources of authority in the community and country.
- Identify patriotic symbols, celebrations, and traditions.
- Compare the past with the present.
- Locate oceans, continents, mountains, islands, and other features on a map or globe.
- Identify a variety of landforms.
- Explore how resources are used to produce goods and services.
- Identify differences in people, cultures, and traditions.

Here are additional topics to consider that help meet the content standards for geography:
- Talk about and identify the seven continents of the world.
- Identify individuals from each country who have made significant contributions to the community and nation, past and present.
- Talk about current events.
- Identify people who provide goods and/or services, and explore different types of local businesses.
- Add map symbols to the globe.

From Jamaica to Japan, South Africa to Scotland and beyond—you will have so much fun crisscrossing the globe, you will not want to return home!

Getting Packed for the Trip

You are about to embark on a great journey—the ultimate field trip around the world! As your class travels across continents and over oceans to visit children around the globe, you will want to keep a log of your experiences in a Travel Journal. Here is what you will need to take care of the wonderful keepsakes and memories of your expeditions:

Storage Folder

Have the children write their names on the outsides of file folders. This is where the children will keep all of their papers until you have finished traveling and are ready to compile the journals. Keep all of the folders together in a safe place.

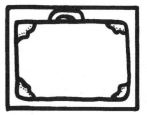

Travel Suitcase

Make two copies of the Travel Suitcase pattern **(page 7)** on heavy card stock for each child. Have the children cut out the suitcases and glue each one onto a 9" x 12" (23 cm x 30 cm) sheet of construction paper. Have them write their names on the front of one suitcase page and on the back of the other—just in case things get lost in transit. After you have visited all of the countries, laminate the completed suitcase pages and place them in the file folder.

Passport

Before you travel, everyone will need a passport. Make a copy of the Passport pattern **(page 8)** on heavy card stock for each child. Cut along the solid lines around the passport book cover. Take a picture of each student and trim the picture to fit inside the book cover. Color the book cover as desired, sign the line provided, glue the child's picture to the inside front cover, and laminate. Fold the passport book cover in half along the dotted lines. Cut several sheets of copy paper (each child will need four sheets) to 4" x 5" (10 cm x 13 cm). Take four pages, fold them in half, and staple them to the inside of the passport book. Place the passport into the file folder.

Globe

Cut two pieces of light blue construction paper by rounding two corners as shown. Glue the light blue semicircles to two separate sheets of 9" x 12" (23 cm x 30 cm) construction paper. Make a copy of the Continents patterns **(pages 9–10)** for each child. Have the children color the continents as desired, cut along the dashed lines, and glue them onto the blue paper. Use a world map or globe for reference to place the continents correctly.

Visiting the Countries

Your class will be learning about a lot of children and their cultures and countries. Here are some suggestions to help you manage all of the paperwork:

- Make a guidebook for each country. Fold several sheets of construction paper in half and staple them together to create a book. Have the children write, "My Guide to [insert name of country]" on their book covers. Then have them fill their books by writing facts or illustrating activities that will help them remember the experiences they had while exploring the country.

- Keep a copy of flags, postcards, and other artwork for the file folder in groups so that all of the papers for each country are compiled together.

- Have the children glue the globe markers on their globes next to the appropriate countries. Have them write the name of each country on the map as you go. Once you have visited all of the countries, laminate the globes.

- Have the children glue the souvenir stickers collected from each country on their travel suitcases. Once you have visited all of the countries, laminate the suitcases. These will become the outside covers of your students' Travel Journals.

- Have the children glue the passport stamps and write the date you visited each country on the appropriate pages in the passport book.

- Have the children color the flag and the pictures of the children in traditional dress for each country. Add these to the travel folders.

Return Flight Home

My Favorite Travel Memory

Once you have visited all of the countries, make a copy of the My Favorite Travel Memory pattern **(page 11)** and My Flag pattern **(page 12)** for each child. Encourage the children to think back on the many things they did and learned. Have each child choose a favorite activity, draw a picture of it, and write or dictate a few sentences about the experience on the My Favorite Travel Memory page. (You may want to create a separate memory page for each country.) Then encourage the children to think about all of the flags they have seen and create their own flags using the My Flag pattern.

Assembling the Travel Book

Place the back side of the Travel Suitcase facedown on the table. Add pages from each country facedown on top of the suitcase. Place the "My Country" and "All About Me" pages facedown on the top of the stack, followed by the "My Favorite Memory" and "My Flag" pages. Place the top half of the travel suitcase on top of the stack and bind all of the pages together. Staple a quart-sized zippered plastic bag to the inside cover of the travel book. Have the children store their postcards and passports inside these bags.

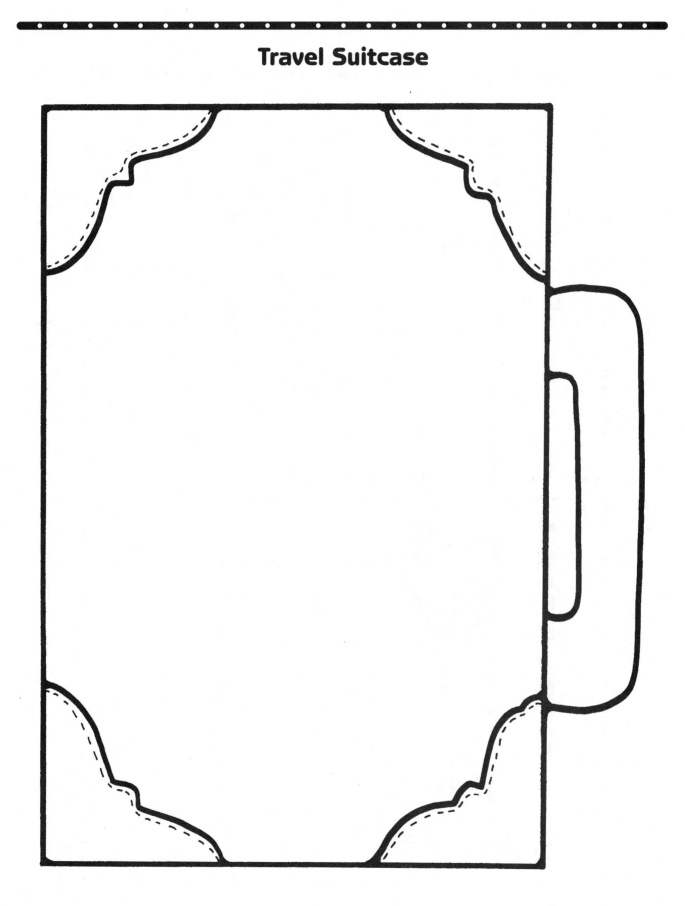

7

Passport

Continents (1)

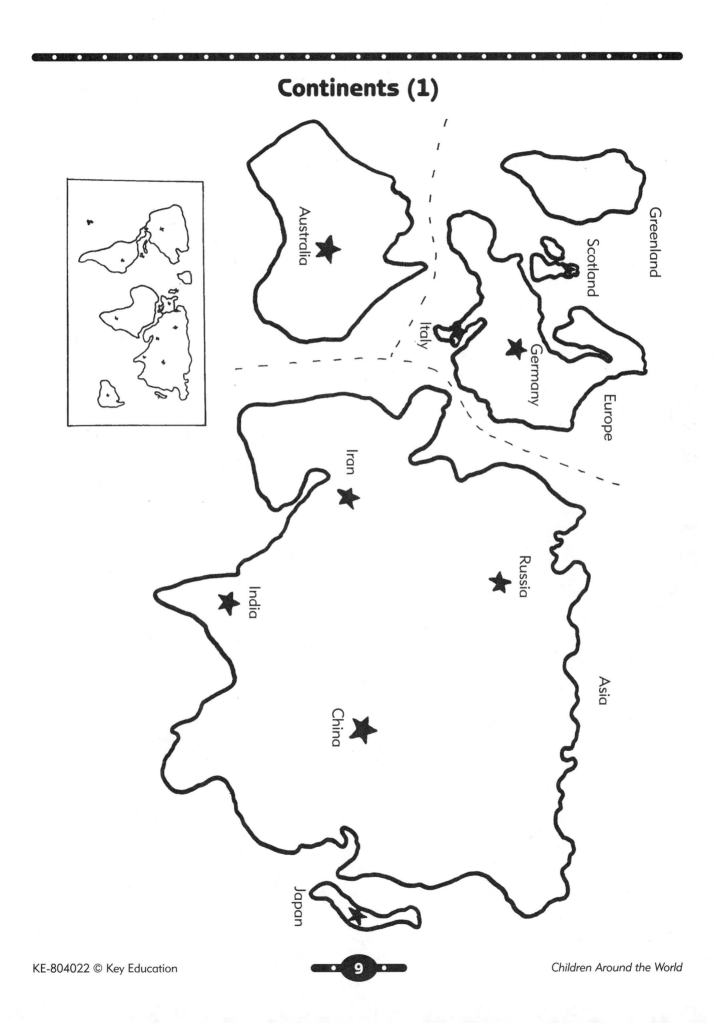

9

Continents (2)

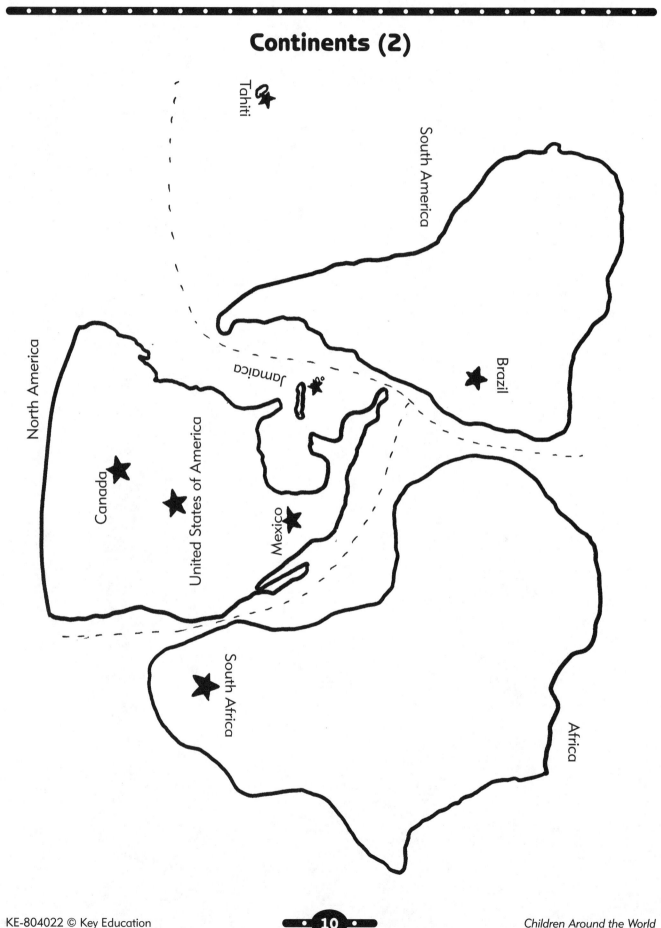

Children Around the World

My Favorite Travel Memory

My Flag

My Country: USA or Canada

Before we embark on our excursion, it may be helpful to get a grasp on where we come from. Many of the things we will learn about on our field trip around the world will be unique and exotic. On the other hand, we will also find that many things are familiar. Start a journal by having each child create a self-portrait and mount it to a sheet of colored construction paper. Have the child write "My Country" across the top of the page and his or her name along the bottom. Add eight more pages behind the first and staple or punch holes and lace with yarn to bind the pages together. Consider each of the following topics for a page in your "My Country" books.

Myself

Each one of us is unique, and each one of us shares similarities with others. What is amazing is that no matter how similar we may be, there are no two of us on the face of the earth who are exactly alike. Have the children write, "I am special" on the second pages of their books and list everything they feel is special about themselves. Encourage the children to add illustrations to the back side of page 1 (opposite their lists), or provide them with one or two snapshots that you or their parents have taken throughout the year to use in decorating their pages.

My Family

A family is made up of two or more people who are related to one another through birth or legal ties. Family members love each other even when they may not live together in the same house. Have the class help you formulate a list of things that families are. Write "Families are . . ." across the top of a sheet of paper. Have all of the children, in turn, write their thoughts on the paper and then sign their names. Make copies for everyone to glue inside their books on page 3. On the back side of page 2 (facing the "Families are . . ." page), have the children write and illustrate ideas of activities they like to do with their families.

Families are different and the same all over the world. The more you study about the world, the more you will find that people of all races and nationalities live all over the world—not just in their home countries. For example, there are many ethnic Chinese who live in Tahiti; South Africa was colonized by people from Europe; and America is known as the melting pot of the world because people from hundreds of nations have come to make it their home. Send a note home with the children requesting that they discuss as a family where their families came from before they lived in America or Canada. Have the children share this information with the rest of the class. Then mark the locations on a world map or make a map as described in the "Getting Packed for Your Trip" section **(page 5)**.

My Friends

Have the children write "My friends" on page 4 of their books. Have them describe their favorite activities to do with friends and illustrate those things on the page.

Talk with the class about how we are all connected to one another in many ways. We have friends from sports teams, friends from school, friends from other classes, and friends from the neighborhood. Just as we have come to know people who live close to us, there will be many people, perhaps from all over the world, that will someday be their friends, too. Consider contacting an educational or Internet resource (or perhaps a teaching colleague in another state or country) to set up a pen-pal exchange for the class. Have all correspondence come to the school so that you can monitor the content and share it together as a class.

My Foods

We all need food to live and grow. In some parts of the world, food is scarce and people work long, hard hours to provide for their families. In other places, food is plentiful. Plan for a favorite foods day where the children can share in a feast of favorite foods brought from home. If your

class is diverse in culture, you may find yourself sampling items from around the world right in your own classroom. Have the children write "My Foods" on page 5 of their books. Using old magazines and catalogs, have the children cut out pictures of favorite foods and glue them onto the page. Help them label each picture and write the names of other foods they love but could not find pictures for.

My Customs

Customs are activities that are usual—things that happen often or even every day. Every country has unique customs regarding clothing, holidays, and activities. For example, ask the children to describe the clothing worn by kids in your school. Chances are they would be able to come up with a fairly consistent list. Often customs are influenced by where we live and by our beliefs. Children who live where it is warm dress differently than children who live in cold climates. Children who live in cold climates enjoy different activities than those who live in warm climates. Some children's dress and activities are governed by religious beliefs. Your best friend may celebrate different holidays than you do even though you live right next door to one another.

Have the children write "My Customs" on page 6 of their books. Ask them to make a list of favorite holidays or activities that are common to their families.

My Home

Every person needs shelter, or a place to live. Homes are another aspect of living that varies with geography, climate, and socioeconomic status. If you live in a big city, you probably live in an apartment or a small home. If you live in the country, you may have a home with a sizable yard or farmland nearby. If you live in the suburbs, chances are you live in an apartment or home that looks very similar to other homes in the area.

Homes around the world differ, too. A home in the Amazon rain forest is made out of sticks, leaves, and branches of Amazon trees. A home in Jamaica might be erected on "borrowed land" (land that does not belong to anyone) and be made out of corrugated metal and plastic. The roofs of many Chinese homes slope steeply and then curl up at the ends. Homes in Japan have paper walls that can be moved when more space is needed. Homes in Norway have sod (grass) on the roof. Some homes are built with the latest technology where a computer can turn the lights on for you before you even get home. Some homes do not have electricity or running water. Obtain as many pictures of homes from around the world as possible (look under the subject of "architecture" in your local library) and share them with your class.

Have the children write "My Home" on page 7 of their books. Then ask them to draw pictures of their homes. Give the children a take-home assignment to explore their homes and consider the materials needed to build it. Have them count the rooms, doors, and windows; estimate how tall the home is; and so forth. Have them add this information to their home pages.

My School, My Community, My Country

School is an important community. Have the children discuss what kinds of things they learn while at school. Discuss the importance of the legislative system by pointing out the freedoms that your children enjoy that other children around the world may not. For example, many children in China do not have siblings because of the laws of the land. In other countries, children may be denied certain rights because of race or gender.

Have the children write "My Country" on page 8 of their books. Ask them to describe what they like best about living in the United States of America or Canada.

Now that you have the journals started, keep them going throughout the course of your travels around the world. Encourage the children to add other thoughts about each subject as they study each different country and culture.

Flag of the U.S.A.

Directions: In the upper left corner make the stars white on a dark blue background. To color the stripes, alternate with red and white.

Flag of the Canada

Directions: Color the stripes of the flag: red, white, and red (left to right). Make the maple leaf red.

Child in Traditional American
Uncle Sam Costume

Children in Traditional Canadian Costumes

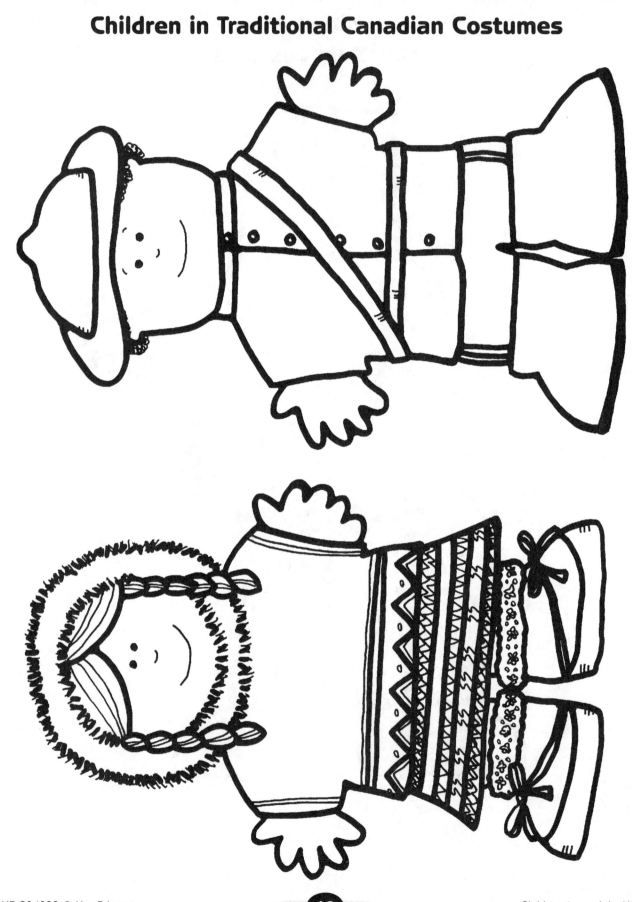

American Postcard, Globe Marker,
Luggage Sticker, and Passport Stamp

Postcard

Globe Marker

USA

Passport Stamp

USA

USA

Luggage Sticker

Canadian Postcard, Globe Marker,
Luggage Sticker, and Passport Stamp

Postcard

Globe
Marker

Canada

Passport Stamp

Luggage
Sticker

Canada

Canada

Australia

Capital: Canberra
Official Language: English

G'day, mate! And welcome to Australia—the "Land down under." Located in the Southern Hemisphere between the Pacific and Indian Oceans, Australia even celebrates Christmas in the summertime (its seasons are opposite of those in the Northern Hemisphere), so Santa visits children from Australia on the beach! From the Great Barrier Reef to the Outback, from bandicoots to wallabies, Australia is a place like no other in the world.

Although Australians speak English, they also have their own special language. Here are a few examples of Aussie slang:

English	Australian English
Children	Ankle biters
Cheer for your team	Barrack for
Lots of money	Big bickies
Container for boiling water	Billy
Man	Bloke
Quarrel/fight	Blue
Swimsuit	Cossie
Genuine/true	Fair dinkum
Rumor/false news	Furphy
Sheep	Jumbuck
Prankster	Larrikin
Candies	Lollies
Buddy	Mate
Journey through the country	On the wallaby
Terrific	Ripper
Throw a tantrum	Spit the dummy
Nosy person	Sticky beak
Hard work	Yakka

For more information about Australia:

Embassy of Australia
1601 Massachusetts Avenue NW
Washington, DC 20036

Phone: (202) 797-3000
Fax: (202) 797-3168
http://www.austemb.org/

Australian Safari

One of the most interesting things about Australia is the abundance of unusual wildlife. Australia is home to the bandicoot, bilby, cockatoo, death adder, dingo, echidna, emu, frilled lizard, kangaroo, koala, kookaburra, platypus, Tasmanian devil, wallaby, wombat, and more! Divide the class into teams and have each team choose an animal from Australia. Allow the teams to use the library and the Internet to research their animals. Have each team draw a picture of their chosen animal and write a couple of sentences about it. Create an "Outback Corner" where the Australian animals can be posted. Help the children make binoculars by stapling two empty toilet tissue rolls together. Attach an 18" (46 cm) string to hang them around the neck and have the children decorate their binoculars as desired. Use the binoculars as you explore each animal on an "Outback Safari."

Extend the activity by creating an Australian Safari Mobile. Make a copy of the Australian Safari Mobile patterns **(pages 26–28)** for each child. Have the children color the shapes and cut them out along the solid black lines. Cut a 24" (61 cm) length of yarn for each child. Have the child tape the "Australian Safari" topper about 4" (10 cm) from the top of the string, then tape each animal picture to the string, leaving 2" (5 cm) between pictures. The box with information about each animal should be glued to the back side of the matching animal picture. Trim off the bottom of the string if necessary and hang the mobiles from the ceiling.

Beach Heaven

Since Australia is surrounded by water, it has many beaches for swimming, sailing, playing in the sand, and enjoying the sunny weather. There are many festivals and celebrations that take place on the beach, and you can always find people in their cossies (swimsuits), cooking on the barbie (barbecue). One celebration is called the Seashore Carnival. Among other games, relays that demonstrate lifesaving skills are played between teams of lifeguards. Each team dresses up in matching uniforms. Two team members swim out into the ocean and pretend that they need help. A third member swims out to the people in the water and "rescues" them while other team members pull those in the water safely to shore with a life ring. The team that can do this most quickly is declared the winner.

Create your own lifesaving relay by tossing a small beach ball a short distance away. Mark a line with masking tape and tie a rope around a doughnut-shaped ring. Have the children stand on the line and try to toss the ring over the beach ball. Once the beach ball has been successfully caught, pull the ball back to the starting line by gently reeling in the swim ring. Extend the activity to try "saving" other objects or balls of different size and composition.

While you are visiting the beach, you can try a little surfing, swimming, or dancing, build sand castles, look for treasures buried in the sand, and enjoy a picnic.

Shark Attack!

With all that water, Australia is home to many sharks, too. Most beaches post signs warning of the dangers of sharks. These signs let beachcombers know where it is safe and not safe to swim.

Play a game of Shark Attack! with your class. Have all of the children line up on one side of the play area. Choose one or two children to be "sharks" and have them stand on the opposite side of the play area. Have these children wear shark hats (see instructions on page 23) to distinguish

themselves from the swimmers. Once the sharks turn their backs, the swimmers can all enter the "water" (play area) and begin swimming toward the sharks. The sharks then turn around, yell "Shark attack!" and chase the swimmers back across the starting line. Swimmers who are "bitten" (tagged) must swim to shore for first aid. Place a bandage (or tie a strip of cloth for a bandage) on the spot where the shark attack occurred. Once everyone has been caught, choose new sharks and begin again.

Use the Shark Hat pattern **(page 29)** to make shark hats for the children. Copy the pattern for each child onto heavy card stock. Draw a dorsal fin pattern (see illustration below) and make two copies for each child. Have each child cut a 2" x 14" (5 cm x 36 cm) strip of construction paper and color the shark fin and jaws as desired. Show the children how to bend the teeth down toward the underside of the jaws along the solid line that separates the teeth from the jaws. Then bend 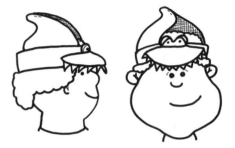 the eyes toward the jaws along the dotted line. Measure the construction paper strip to fit each child's head and staple the ends together to make a headband. Have each child glue the fins to either side of the headband and then glue or staple them together at the tip of the fin. The eyes should be glued to the front of the headband so that the jaw extends over the front of the forehead. Encourage the children to wear their shark hats while playing beach games or eating lunch.

Opera House

While you are close to shore, enjoy the Opera House in Sydney. It was built to look like sailboats on the water. Bring in a picture of the Sydney Opera House and have the children offer suggestions for what they think it looks like.

Explain that operas—plays in which the words are sung rather than spoken—are performed in this famous building. Have the children put on an opera of a familiar story, such as "The Three Bears." Find costumes and props as necessary, and have the children act out the play by singing the lines rather than reciting them.

Great Barrier Reef

Just off the northeast coastline of Australia lies the Great Barrier Reef, home to an unparalleled array of fish, coral, and other sea life. Create your own reef in the classroom by placing a large sheet of blue craft paper on the floor. Have the children use watercolor paints to depict the sea life that lives in and around a coral reef.

Outback

The Outback is located in south central Australia. It is hot and dry and home to many of the creatures you learned about in the Australian Safari activity. Because it is so hot and dry, most of the animals prefer to be underground during the day and only come out after the sun is down. Even some of the people who live in the heart of the Outback live in underground homes. Many of the children who live in this region live too far away from school to attend. They get their lessons in the mail and then talk to their teachers via two-way radios.

Place one copy of a worksheet or word search puzzle in an envelope for each child. Address the envelopes and place them all in a large mailbox in your classroom. As the children remove their envelopes throughout the day, have them "call" you on a set of walkie-talkies to discuss the assignment. Just like the children in the Outback, you can communicate back and forth with each child using the radios.

Uluru

Right in the middle of Australia is Uluru (formerly known as Ayers Rock). Uluru is a monolith, which means it is one large rock. Visitors to the Outback enjoy exploring this rock because of its massive size and because it appears to change colors throughout the day as the sun's rays shine upon it. Aborigines (a group of native Australians) believe that Uluru is a sacred place. Their drawings and paintings can be found inside the caves and all over the face of the rock.

Create your own monolith in the classroom. Cover the underside of a large table with craft paper. Then wrap the outside of the table in another piece of craft paper, leaving a small space on one side open so the children can climb in and out of the cave. Provide chalk so the children can create cave drawings and other aboriginal art on the sides, wall, and top of the monolith.

Aborigines

The Aborigines are a group of people who lived in Australia long before the European settlers began inhabiting the land. The Aboriginal people live off the land and move from place to place to hunt and find food. Long ago, Aborigines were considered lesser-class citizens and were removed from some of their lands. Today Australia recognizes the Aborigines' right to their own way of life and is less obtrusive in their lives.

Aborigines teach their children the dances and folklore of their heritage. Wearing beaded necklaces, grass skirts, and painted bodies, the Aborigines share their stories through song and dance. Prepare for your own classroom Aboriginal celebration with the activities listed below:

- Place a small circle of large rocks in the center of the room for a fire ring.

- Have the children create beaded necklaces out of a variety of pastas.

- Make grass skirts by running strips of 2" (5 cm) wide masking tape along the long edges of pieces of newspaper. Extend the tape 12" (30 cm) on each end and fold in half so there are no sticky sides showing. Have the children fringe the skirts by cutting straight strips from the free end of the newspaper up to the tape. Tie the skirts around the children's waists.

- A didgeridoo is a long, hollow, wooden tube that makes low sounds when you blow into it. It is typically played by Aboriginal elders and painted with Aboriginal artwork. To make your own didgeridoos, cut 2' (61 cm) lengths of PVC piping, or gather paper towel or wrapping paper tubes—one for each child. Have the children decorate the outsides of their tubes with colorful lines and dots. Encourage them to blow into the tubes to make music.

- Check out a book of Aboriginal folklore from the library or read a favorite excerpt from books such as *What Made Tiddalik Laugh* by Joanna Troughton (Peter Bedrick Books, 1986) or *Dreamtime: Aboriginal Stories* by Oodgeroo (Lothrop, Lee & Shepard, 1994).

- Have the children make up a dance to go with a story and have them dance, clap, and play their didgeridoos around the campfire.

- Extend the didgeridoo activity by creating a set of didgeridoos that are different lengths and widths. Ask the children to listen carefully and decide which instruments make the lowest and highest sounds. Experiment with one didgeridoo, cutting off the end 2" (5 cm) at a time to demonstrate how the pitch gets higher when the tube is shorter.

Aboriginal Painting

Aboriginal paintings depict bold, natural colors as well as geometric figures and shapes. Although primitive in look, Aboriginal art is quite popular and is sold all over the world. Using paint and craft paper, have the children create their own Aboriginal artwork. (You may want to check out a book depicting the art form from the library or look to online sources for samples of the Aboriginal style of painting.) Frame each masterpiece and use to decorate the classroom.

Sheep Station

Wool and mutton exports are a big part of the Australian economy, and there are many, many sheep stations (ranches) around the country. Just as the name is a little bit different, the cowboys in Australia also herd the sheep a little differently. To get around the large sheep stations, Australian sheep ranchers use motorbikes instead of horses.

Knowing how many head of sheep are in your herd is an important part of the job for a sheep rancher. Prepare a sheet of math sentences appropriate to the grade level of your class. Then give each child a herd of sheep in the form of a bag and a handful of cotton balls. The child's job is to move the sheep from the fields into the pen by following the instructions on the math page. For example, if problem #1 says 2 + 4, the child should count out two cotton ball sheep and then four more. After adding them together, the child may write down the sum and move the sheep into the bag. The child continues counting sheep until they are all safely in the "pen."

Pavlova

Pavlova is a favorite Australian treat. Make the pavlova together as a class and then enjoy them for an afternoon snack.

2 egg whites
1/2 tsp. (2.5 mL) cream of tartar
2/3 c. (160 mL) sugar
1/2 tsp. (2.5 mL) vanilla

Let the egg whites stand at room temperature for 30 minutes. Add cream of tartar and beat until soft peaks form. Add sugar and vanilla gradually, beating on high speed until stiff peaks form and sugar is nearly dissolved. Spread the meringue into a circle on a parchment-lined or lightly greased baking sheet. Press down on the center to form a bowl in the meringue. Bake at 300°F for 35 minutes. Turn off the oven and let the shell dry with the door closed for one hour. Remove the shell from the baking sheet and fill it with fresh fruit and whipped cream.

Australian Safari Mobile (1)

Kangaroo

A kangaroo hops on its strong legs and balances with its tail. The mother has a pocket on her belly where the baby joey sleeps and eats.

Platypus

A platypus is a mammal that lays eggs. It swims underwater with its eyes closed and strains food through its duck-like bill.

Termites

Termites chew on wood for food. They build tall nest mounds that can grow to 6 feet high (1.82 m) or higher.

Australian Safari

Australian Safari Mobile (2)

Koala

A koala is a nocturnal animal that prefers solitude and eats eucalyptus leaves.

Dingo

A dingo is a wild dog. It usually eats rodents. Dingoes do not bark, but howl instead.

Frilled Lizard

When it is startled or threatened, the frilled lizard opens up the frill in its neck to make itself look bigger. It will also show its teeth and hiss when alarmed.

Bandicoot

A bandicoot is a nocturnal marsupial. It has a long nose and hops on its hind legs. Bandicoots fight with their hind legs and only bite if they have to.

Australian Safari Mobile (3)

Wombat

A wombat is a grass-eating marsupial. It uses its front legs to dig burrows in the ground where it lives.

Echidna

An echidna is a spiny animal that burrows into the ground when frightened. It has a long beak, sharp claws, and a sticky tongue for eating ants, termites, and worms.

Kookaburra

A kookaburra is a bird that eats snakes, mice, insects, and sometimes fish. The kookaburra lives in tree holes, and its call sounds like a laugh.

Inland Taipan

The Inland Taipan is the world's deadliest snake. Just a tiny bit of its venom can kill thousands of mice.

Shark Hat

Children in Traditional Australian Dress

Flag of Australia

Directions: Color the small British Union flag red, white, and blue. Make the stars white on a blue background.

Australian Postcard, Globe Marker, Luggage Sticker, and Passport Stamp

Postcard

Globe Marker

Australia

Passport Stamp

Luggage Sticker

Brazil

Capital: Brasilia
Official Language: Portuguese

Brazil is one of the largest countries in the world. It is located on the east coast of South America. Brazil is home to the Amazon Rain Forest and the Amazon River. Although the people of Brazil know how to work hard to provide for their families, they also know how to play hard, too.

Enjoy the celebrations and wonders to be found in Brazil! Here are a few Portuguese words and phrases to help you get started:

English	Portuguese
Hello	Oi / Olá
Good-bye	Tchau
Thank you	Obrigado
Peace	Paz
1 – one	um
2 – two	dois
3 – three	três
4 – four	quatro
5 – five	cinco
6 – six	seis
7 – seven	sete
8 – eight	oito
9 – nine	nove
10 – ten	dez

For more information about Brazil:

Brazilian Embassy
3006 Massachusetts Avenue NW
Washington, DC 20008

Phone: (202) 238-2700
Fax: (202) 238-2827
http://www.brasilemb.org/

Cattle, Pigs, and Chickens

While Brazil also has large modern cities, many Brazilians live on farms to support their families. Cattle, pigs, and chickens are the most common animals raised by gauchos, or Brazilian cowboys.

Make several copies of the Cattle, Pigs, and Chickens Game Cards pattern **(page 38)** on card stock. Cut out the game cards along the solid lines and laminate the cards. To play the game, deal all of the cards facedown to two players. Each player turns over the top card from his stack at the same time. If one of the cards is a cow, the player with the cow collects both cards and places them in a discard pile. If one of the cards is a pig and the other a chicken, the player with the pig collects both cards and places them in her discard pile. Cows beat pigs and chickens, pigs beat chickens, and chickens lose every time. If both players turn over the same animal card, the players must stand up, make the sound of that animal, spin around once, and return to their seats. For example, if two cows are laid on the table, both players stand up and say "moo" while turning a circle. The first player to sit back down collects both cards. If there is a tie, each player takes his own card and places it in his discard pile. Play continues until one person is out of cards.

Sugarcane Plantations

One of Brazil's most important crops is sugarcane. Brazilian sugarcane is harvested and made into sugar products for export all over the world. Try this fun science experiment and grow your own sugar crystals.

1/2 c. (120 mL) pure cane sugar	cellophane tape
1 c. (240 mL) hot water	glass jar or plastic cup
food coloring (optional)	wooden skewer

Dissolve cane sugar in hot water by stirring sugar into the water one spoonful at a time. Continue adding sugar and stirring until the solution is saturated and no more sugar can be dissolved. Add two or three drops of food coloring if desired. Stretch a piece of tape over the mouth of a glass jar or plastic cup. Gently poke a wooden skewer through the tape into the sugar solution so that it is immersed in the sugar but not touching the bottom of the glass. Place the glass in a safe place where it will not get bumped or spilled. Observe the crystals forming over the next few days. Once the skewer is covered in crystals, remove it from the solution and enjoy. Notice that the crystals are the same size and shape, and while they taste just like the sugar granules you stirred into the solution, they look quite different.

Amazon Rain Forest

The famous Amazon River flows through the Amazon Rain Forest. This rain forest is home to many different species of animals, trees, plants, and insects, as well as a few groups of humans. In fact, the forest is so dense with plant and animal life, scientists are still discovering new species today. Here are some activities to enjoy while exploring the Amazon Rain Forest in Brazil:

- Decorate your classroom to look like a rain forest. Make several tree trunks by twisting long strips of brown craft paper and stapling or taping them to the walls. Cover the tops

of the walls and the ceiling with huge leaves cut from green craft paper. Add vines made from thin strips of green and brown craft paper that has been twisted into ropes. Drape the vines and even more leaves across the ceiling. Add other plants, ferns, and mosses throughout the room. Talk about the different layers of the rain forest (emergent layer, canopy, understory, and forest floor) and the types of animals and plants that can be found in each.

- Have the children learn about the different kinds of animals that live in a rain forest, such as the anaconda, macaw, poison dart frog, caiman, peccary, leaf-cutter ant, and anteater. Ask them to illustrate each animal they study, and hang their illustrations on the walls and ceiling throughout your rain forest.

- Obtain a CD of sounds or music from the rain forest. Play it quietly in the background to create atmosphere for your rain forest.

- Ask the children to pretend they are scientists exploring the Amazon rain forest. Have each child think up a new species of plant or animal that has just been discovered. Make one copy of the Amazon Daily Gazette pattern **(page 39)** for each child. Have the children draw pictures of their newly discovered plants or animals and then write a few sentences about their discoveries in the space provided on the page. Encourage them to be creative and to include details such as what the animal might eat or what kinds of creatures might live in or eat the plant. Mount the completed pages on sheets of newspaper cut to 11" x 13" (28 cm x 33 cm), and hang the discoveries on the wall of the classroom or in the hall for all to enjoy.

- Play a game of Amazon Charades. Write the names of several Amazon rain forest animals on index cards, or obtain pictures of a variety of the animals. Have one child act out each animal name using movement and sound, if necessary, until the other children guess which animal it is.

Brazilian Indians

There are many groups of Indians still living in the Amazon rain forest today. Most of these groups have little or no contact with the outside world. The lives of the children in these groups are much different than the lives of children in our own country. For example, rather than learning to ride a bike, these children learn to paddle a boat on their own by the time they are old enough to start school. Most children do not wear shoes on their feet in the Amazon rain forest—shoes just get caked with mud and become a nuisance. These children may have parrots or boa constrictors for pets. (Dogs are used for hunting.) There is no fast food, so every meal is hunted or fished for and then cooked over a fire. There is no television, no electricity, no stores, no beds, and no video games. Ask the children in your class to imagine what their lives would be like if they could change places with children in the Amazon.

Indians of the Amazon rain forest often fashion headbands out of reeds, twigs, leaves, and feathers found on the forest floor. Help the children create their own headbands by following the directions on the next page.

Cut 2" x 12" (5 cm x 30 cm) strips of construction paper. You will need two per child. Cut several straws to 2" (5 cm) lengths. Gather twigs, leaves, blades of grass, and feathers, and place the materials in separate containers. Have the children assemble their headbands by first laying one strip of paper flat on the table. Have them glue the cut straws vertically along their headbands so that the open ends are even with the sides of the construction paper strips. Then have them spread glue across the exposed sides of the straws and press the second paper strip on top so that it lines up with the first strip. Help the children tape the ends of the two strips together to enclose the straws and then punch two holes in each end through the tape. Lay the headbands flat while they dry completely. Once the glue is dry, have the children poke sticks, leaves, twigs, or feathers into the straw pieces, gluing the materials in place if necessary. Show the children how to thread one 12" (30 cm) length of string through each end of the headband and tie the headbands around their heads. Enjoy wearing your headbands as you fish or dance while beating drums.

Spearfishing

One way to get food in the Amazon is by fishing. In places where the river is too narrow to use nets, people use a method of fishing called spearfishing. Fishermen stand in the river and spear or poke through the fish with long, sharp sticks. Make several copies of the Spearfishing pattern **(page 40)** on different colored paper. Cut out the fish shapes and scatter them around a carpeted playing area. Have the children use wooden skewers to spear the fish in order from 1 to 10, stacking the fish on their skewers. Alternatively, make up cards with different math sentences and divide the class into pairs. Have one child from each pair call out the math sentence (e.g., 7 – 6 =) and the other child spear the fish that matches the answer (e.g., 1).

Piranhas

While fishing, you have to look out for piranhas. Piranhas are small fish, but they are very ferocious. They swim in large packs and will devour anything that gets in their way. Cut out large boulder shapes (about 3' in diameter) using gray, black, or brown craft paper. You will need one boulder for every three students in the class. Place the boulders around the perimeter of the play area. Then have the children stand inside the ring of boulders, pretending to swim in the Amazon River. When you call "Piranha attack!" the children should run to safety and stand on a boulder to get out of the water. The trick is to get as many children as possible onto each boulder shape so that no one is eaten by the piranhas. After each piranha attack, remove one boulder and play again. The game gets more and more challenging as the number of boulders decreases.

Brazilian Celebrations

Brazil has many special celebrations throughout the year. Read below to learn about two of the more popular holidays and some suggestions for celebrating them.

Festa de Lemanjá — This festival is celebrated in Rio de Janeiro to pay honor to the goddess

of the sea. The people wear long white robes and necklaces of glass beads. They place lighted candles in the sand at darkness on December 31 (or in February in other places in Brazil) and toss perfume, beads, and fruit into the waves as presents to the sea goddess. Some people fill baskets with these presents and row them out to sea. Those who believe the legend say that if the basket of presents sinks, the giver's wishes will be granted.

- Bead necklaces—Encourage everyone to wear white on the day you celebrate this holiday, and provide clear beads and string for making necklaces.

- Glass candleholders—Collect several small glass baby food jars, one for each student. Let the children use glass paints (found in craft stores) to decorate their jars with bright colors and designs. Encourage the children to light their jars at home with adult supervision by placing small candles inside the jars.

- Sinking baskets—In an outside play area, fill a small wading pool with water. Set a plastic bucket or basket in the water. Place several other objects, such as balls and sticks, in a separate bucket outside of the pool. Have the children work in teams to try to sink the basket by tossing objects into it.

Carnaval — The Brazilian *carnaval* is perhaps the biggest celebration of the year. It is celebrated six days before Ash Wednesday. (Ash Wednesday is the start of the Lenten season for those of Catholic faith.) There are big parades, performances by samba dancers, colorful costumes, confetti, streamers, drums, and trumpets. Many of the floats in the parade are made with huge papier-mâché statues.

- Samba—Collect a selection of samba music. Make flower leis and dance away!

- Feathered masks—Help the children cut eyeholes out of the middle of paper plates. Then have them cover their plates with colorful feathers, leaving the eyeholes clear. Glue craft sticks to the bottoms of the plates and hold your masks in front of your faces during your *carnaval* parade.

- Papier-mâché statues—Use liquid starch, cardboard boxes and tubes, and strips of newspaper to create colorful papier-mâché statues. Look to the animals of the rain forest for inspiration. Have the children begin by building forms out of cardboard boxes and tubes. Then have them dip newspaper strips into liquid starch and wrap the cardboard forms. Once the forms are dry, have the children paint them with bright colors.

- Fried plantains—Plantains grow abundantly in Brazil. Enjoy this recipe of fried plantains as you celebrate the culture of Brazil.

  2 plantains
  1 tbsp. (15 mL) butter
  cinnamon
  sugar

  Peel and cut plantains in half lengthwise. Fry plantains in butter and then sprinkle with cinnamon and sugar to taste. Let cool a bit before serving.

Cattle, Pigs, and Chickens Game Cards

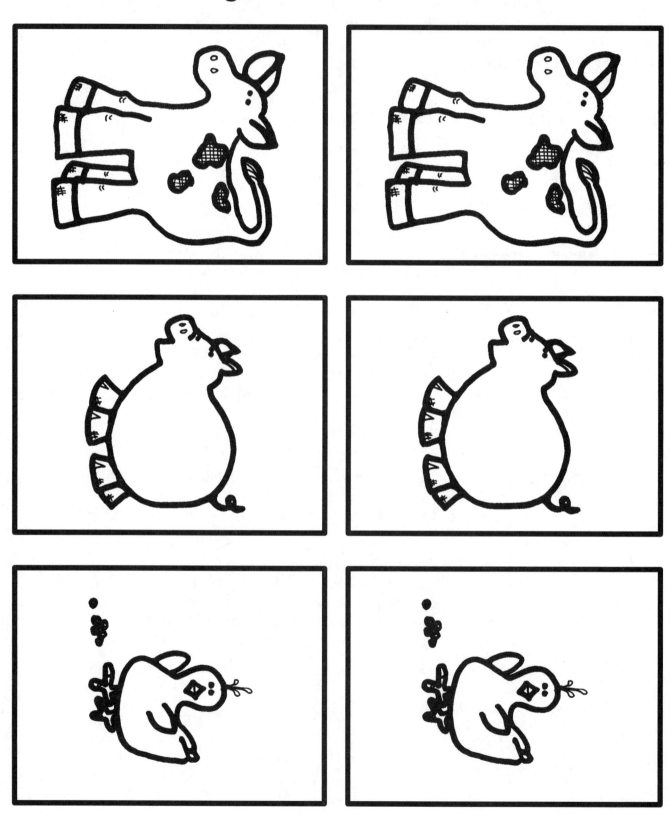

Amazon Daily Gazette

New Species Discovered!

Spearfishing

Children in Traditional Brazilian Dress

Flag of Brazil

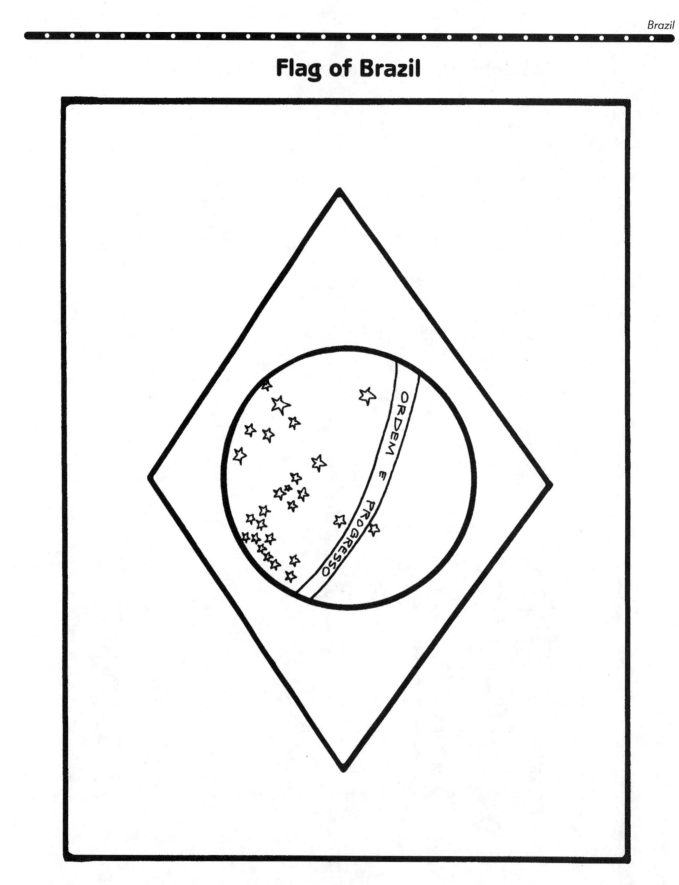

Directions: Color the diamond gold on the green flag. Color the circle blue and the stars and the "ordem e progresso" line white.

Brazilian Postcard, Globe Marker,
Luggage Sticker, and Passport Stamp

Postcard

Luggage
Sticker

Passport
Stamp

Globe
Marker

China

Capital: Beijing
Official Language: Mandarin Chinese

China is located in eastern Asia. It is the third largest country in the world and is also the most populous. Because of the large population, most families in China are allowed to have only one child. Children often live with or near their grandparents and other extended family members, and parents typically live with their children when they get older.

In China, it is considered important to eat well. When two people greet one another, the Chinese often use a phrase that literally means "Have you eaten?" rather than "How are you?" Here are a few Mandarin words and phrases to help you get started on your journey:

English	Mandarin Chinese
Hello	Nǐ hǎo
Good-bye	Zàijiàn
Please	Qǐng
Thank you	Xièxie
Sorry / Excuse me	Duìbuqǐ
1 – one	yī
2 – two	èr
3 – three	sān
4 – four	sì
5 – five	wǔ
6 – six	liù
7 – seven	qī
8 – eight	bā
9 – nine	jiǔ
10 – ten	shí

For more information about China:

Embassy of the People's Republic of China
2300 Connecticut Ave NW
Washington, DC 20008

Phone: (202) 328-2500
Fax: (202) 588-0032
http://www.china-embassy.org/

Land of the Dragon

In China the symbol of the dragon conjures up pleasant thoughts. Dragons are thought to bring abundance, prosperity, and good fortune. Use the Chinese Dragon pattern **(page 49)** to make paper-bag puppets to carry with you throughout your visit to China.

Give each child a copy of the pattern and a paper bag. Have the children color and cut out the dragons along the solid black lines. Then have them glue the dragons' heads to the bottom flaps of the paper bags, coloring the rest of the dragons' bodies with vibrant colors. Model how to attach 12" (30 cm) paper streamers around the top edges of the bags. Slip your hands inside the finished bags and watch the streamers flutter as you dance about with your dragons. If desired, have the children share their dragons with friends to wish each other good luck and prosperity.

Chinese Hats

Chinese farmers often wear wide-brimmed, cone-shaped hats. These hats are great for blocking the sun while working outside in the hot rice paddies.

To make your own hats for your visit to China, cut 2" x 18"(5 cm x 46 cm) strips of red construction paper, one for each child. Fit one strip to each child's head and staple the ends together to make a hatband. Punch one hole each on opposite sides of the hatband and attach a 12" (30 cm) length of string to each hole. Cut two 1" x 12" (2.5 cm x 30 cm) strips of red construction paper for each hat. Staple the strips to the hatband so they criss-cross over the top. **(See illustration.)** Make a circle 18" (46 cm) in diameter out of red craft paper, cutting out a 6" (15 cm) wide pie wedge from the edge to the middle of the circle. Discard the wedge.

Make a copy of the Chinese Zodiac pattern **(page 50)** for each child. Have the children cut out the figures and glue them on their red circles as desired. Then have them finish decorating their hats using markers or crayons.

Show the children how to fold the two edges of the circle together to create a cone, then staple or glue the edges together. Gently place the cones on top of the hatband frames created earlier, and glue or tape the cones to the criss-crossed strips attached to the hatband. Tie the hats under your chins and enjoy!

Chinese New Year

One of the most important holidays in Chinese culture is Chinese New Year. This celebration occurs sometime in January or February, depending on the lunar calendar **(see page 47, Lunar Calendar activities)**. Chinese New Year begins on the first day of the new moon and ends 15 days later with a Lantern Festival on the day of the full moon. Each of the 15 days in the New Year's celebration holds special significance and has specific activities associated with it.

Many traditions and customs are observed during the Chinese New Year celebration. One of the central activities is honoring ancestors. Houses are cleaned, new clothes are donned, debts are paid, and doors and windows are opened to allow the old year out of the house. Houses are decorated with vases of blossoms, tangerines, and happy wishes written on red paper. Special foods that symbolize wealth, health, good fortune, and family togetherness are shared. Children collect money in red envelopes, and everyone enjoys the parades, fireworks, and foods of the day.

Here are some fun activities to help you celebrate the Chinese New Year:

- Encourage the children to wear red (Chinese color of luck) on the first day of the New Year. Cover the door with red paper to bring good luck and fortune to your classroom.

- Make firecrackers by decorating clean, plastic milk jugs with permanent markers or gel pens. (Make sure the jugs have pop-off lids rather than screw-off lids.) Glue a few strands of curling ribbon to the lid of each jug. Fill the bottom of the jug with water and drop two antacid tablets inside. Quickly place the lid on the jug and stand back to watch the fireworks explode into the air.

- Make small envelopes by cutting 4" (10 cm) squares of red construction paper. Fold all four corners in to the center of each square and tape three of them together. Have the children write their names on the envelopes and put them on their desks. When the children are out of the room, slip a small coin into each envelope and seal the last corners shut with tape.

- Make a large paper dragon to parade around the school. Begin by taking a flattened paper grocery bag and cutting off one-third of the bag lengthwise. Decorate the bag to look like a dragon's head using the Chinese Dragon pattern **(page 49)**. Attach a 2' x 35' (0.61 m x 10.7 m) strip of craft paper to the back of the dragon mask—you will need approximately 18" (46 cm) of paper for each child. Glue 2' (61 cm) strips of colored crepe paper along the sides of the craft paper strip. Have one child be the head of the dragon, wearing the paper bag on his head and holding on to the sides of the bag. Have the rest of the class line up underneath the body of the dragon, holding up the paper strip trailing behind the dragon's head. Parade through the halls of school in your dragon costume.

- Write happy wishes such as "Good luck to you" or "You will be happy" on sheets of red paper and post them around the room.

- Have the children write letters to grandparents, aunts, uncles, or parents thanking them for the good fortune that they bring to their families.

- Make lanterns **(see page 56, St. Martin's Day celebration)** and parade through the classroom while banging gongs (foil pie pans), drums (cardboard boxes covered in red paper), and cymbals (pan lids).

Lunar Calendar

Many countries around the world follow a lunar calendar. The moon goes through eight phases, beginning with a new moon, waxing to a full moon, and then waning back to a new moon. This cycle takes approximately 29 days, so a lunar month is shorter than most months of the year. Teach the children about the moon's phases—new moon, waxing crescent, first quarter, waxing gibbous, full moon, waning gibbous, last quarter, and waning crescent—and have them keep a lunar journal for one month. After the month is up, have the children use the information from their journals to predict when the next full moon will occur. Mark it on next month's calendar and have a special moon celebration during the next full moon.

Chinese Zodiac

The Chinese Zodiac consists of 12 animals. Each animal represents a year, repeating every 12 years. For example, the year 2000 was the Year of the Dragon. The next Year of the Dragon will be 2012. The Chinese Zodiac is used to tell fortunes and to determine who is (and is not) most compatible for friendship, marriage, and employment. Part of the Chinese Zodiac's appeal is that it pairs animals based on strengths and weaknesses. For example, a person born in the year of the Goat is compatible with someone born in the year of the Rabbit. The rabbit purportedly has skills and talents that make up for or enhance the strengths or weaknesses of the goat. Refer to the table below to determine what animal represents each of the children in your class. (**See** http://www.chinavoc.com/zodiac **for more information.)**

Year	Animal	Attributes
2008	Rat	Imaginative, charming, generous
2009	Ox	Leader, conservative, good with hands
1998, 2010	Tiger	Sensitive, emotional, loving
1999, 2011	Rabbit	Affectionate, pleasant
2000, 2012	Dragon	Enthusiastic, intelligent, perfectionist
2001, 2013	Snake	Wise, charming, deep thinker
2002, 2014	Horse	Hard worker, independent, friendly
2003, 2015	Goat	Charming, elegant, artistic
2004, 2016	Monkey	Intelligent, witty
2005, 2017	Rooster	Hard worker, decisive, dreamer
2006, 2018	Dog	Loyal, honest, faithful
2007, 2019	Pig	Friendly, sincere, honest

Zodiac Tag

Since most of the children in your class will probably fall into one or two zodiac signs only, assign them random zodiac signs for this game. Make enough copies of the Zodiac Cards pattern **(page 50)** so that there is one card for each child plus one extra complete set of zodiac cards. Punch a hole in each of the student's zodiac cards and tie a 24" (61 cm) length of string through the hole to make a necklace.

To begin play, have each child put on a zodiac necklace. Arrange enough chairs for all but one of the children in a circle. Choose one child to be "It" and have the others sit down in the circle. Draw two cards (e.g., Ox and Rabbit). Announce the names of the animals. The child who is "It" disregards his zodiac animal card until he joins the circle. All children with the two animals named must get up and exchange places before the child who is "It" steals one of their seats. The child with no seat becomes the new "It." Continue drawing cards and swapping seats as time and interest allow.

The Great Wall of China

Many years ago, the Emperor of China ordered the construction of a wall in order to stop advancing armies from invading China. The Great Wall took many, many years to complete. It was created by joining several independent walls together and is more than 4,160 miles (6.693 kilometers) long. Much of the wall is over 2,000 years old and has crumbled in many places.

Have the children work in pairs. Using small wooden blocks, have each pair build a replica of the Great Wall across a desk. The wall should be at least four or five blocks high. Have the children in each pair take turns rolling a die and removing as many blocks as indicated on the face of the die. The object of the game is to weaken the wall enough so that it will collapse during the other child's turn. Encourage the children to look for challenging pieces that may weaken their structures for the next round.

Taoism

One of the more common religious beliefs in China is Taoism. People who practice Taoism try to live in harmony with their natural surroundings. They meditate often, adhere to a vegetarian diet, practice breathing exercises, and engage in *taijiquan* (Tai Chi Chuan). Taijiquan is more commonly known as Tai Chi, an activity in which the movements are intended to strengthen the body and bring the mind into harmony with the body. It is not uncommon to find many people in China in public parks practicing Tai Chi together.

Have the children sit peacefully on the ground and take a few minutes to meditate. Encourage them to breathe slowly and clear their heads of worries. Check out a video on Tai Chi from your local library and try a few of the exercises together as a class.

Yin/Yang Cookies

The symbol for the concept of Yin and Yang is made up of two teardrop shapes that mold together to form a circle (**see illustration**). Yin represents the feminine, cold, and wet, while Yang represents the masculine, hot, and dry. Following Taoist beliefs, every living thing has vital energy, or *chi*. This energy is at its most productive when the yin and yang are in proper balance. As a class, make a list of opposites such as cold/hot, high/low, and boy/girl. Then make yin/yang cookies as directed below. Who knows—you may even improve your chi by eating them!

Cake mix (chocolate or white)
1/2 c. (120 mL) canola oil
1 egg

You will need to make two batches of dough—one chocolate and one white. Make each batch of dough separately, using the ingredients listed above for each batch. Begin with the chocolate cake mix. Combine cake mix, oil, and egg in a bowl and mix thoroughly. Divide dough into balls so that there is at least one ball for each child in the class. Repeat with the white cake mix. Take a ball of white dough and a ball of chocolate dough and gently press together to create one ball of the two. Place dough balls on baking sheet so that half of the white and half of the chocolate dough can be seen. Bake at 350 °F for 12 to 15 minutes.

Chinese Dragon

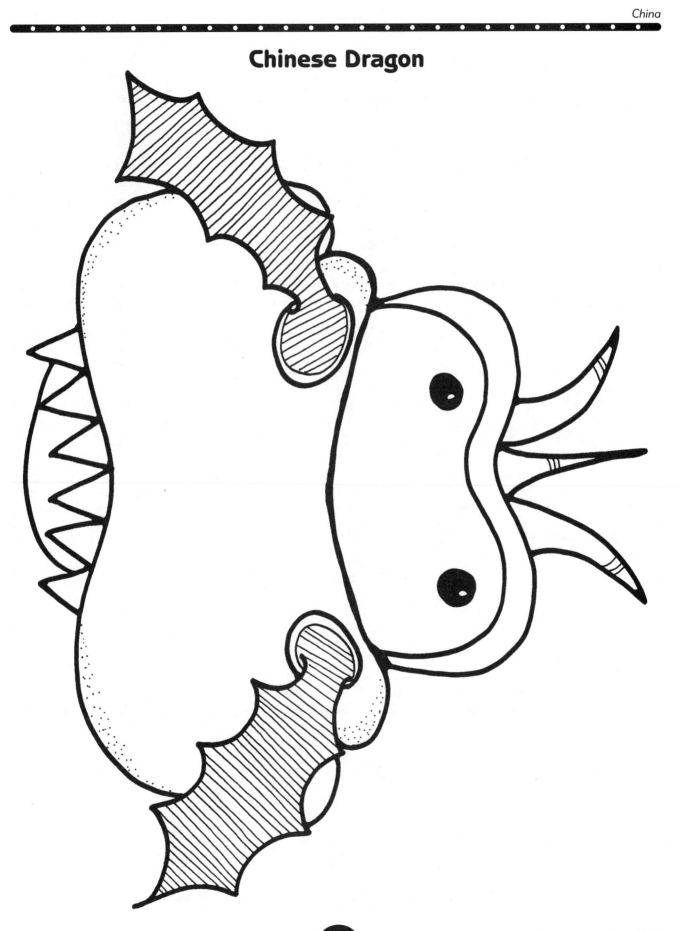

Zodiac Cards

50

Children in Traditional Chinese Dress

Flag of China

Directions: Color the flag red and the stars yellow.

Chinese Postcard, Globe Marker,
Luggage Sticker, and Passport Stamp

Postcard

Globe Marker

China

Luggage Sticker

福
China

Passport Stamp

Germany

Capital: Berlin
Official Language: German

Willkommen in Deutschland! Welcome to Germany! Germany is located in the middle of Europe. It shares borders with nine different countries. Germany used to be divided into two separate states, but they officially reunited in 1989. Put on your *Lederhosen* (traditional leather shorts) and enjoy your visit to Germany!

Here are a few German words and phrases to help you get started on your journey:

English	German
Good day	*Guten Tag*
Hi	*Hallo*
How are you?	*Wie geht's?*
Good-bye	*Auf Wiedersehen*
Please	*Bitte*
Thank you	*Danke*
Yes	*Ja*
No	*Nein*
1 – one	*eins*
2 – two	*zwei*
3 – three	*drei*
4 – four	*vier*
5 – five	*fünf*
6 – six	*sechs*
7 – seven	*sieben*
8 – eight	*acht*
9 – nine	*neun*
10 – ten	*zehn*

For more information about Germany:

German Embassy
4645 Reservoir Road NW
Washington, DC 20007-1998

Phone: (202) 298-4000
Fax: (202) 298-4249 or 333-2653
http://www.germany-info.org/

Black Forest

Germany's Black Forest gets its name from the many fir trees that dot the countryside. The trees are a dark green, making them look almost black. Cuckoo clocks are carved from the wood of these trees and are handcrafted by the people who live in the hills of the Black Forest. A cuckoo clock is unique because a small bird comes out of a door in the clock and "cuckoos" to mark the hour. Other small figures are often incorporated into the clock, and they dance and sing to music that is played on the hour and half hour. A cuckoo clock is wound by pulling on a weighted chain.

Practice telling time by crafting your own cuckoo clocks. Make a copy of the Cuckoo Clock pattern **(page 59)** for each child on heavy card stock. Have the children color their clocks as desired. Cut out the clocks, time cards, doors, clock hands, and weights. Cut along the top and bottom dotted lines on the small rectangle at the bottom of each clock. Fold the doors back along the dotted lines and glue them to the clock so the cuckoo bird is hiding behind the doors. Press a paper brad through both hands of the clock. Attach the hands to the face of the clock by pressing the brad through the center of the clock, indicated by a small dot. Cut drinking straws into 2" (5 cm) pieces. Tape one straw piece about 1/2" (13 mm) from the bottom of the clock on the back side of the clock face. Slip a 12" (30 cm) length of string through the straw and attach the weights to the each end of the string. Slip the time card through the top slits in the rectangle at the bottom of the clock face. The top and bottom of the card should be visible behind the clock. From the back of the clock, move the time card up and down to reveal different times. Move the hands on the clock to match the time shown in the box.

Kindergarten

One German word that is commonly used in English is *kindergarten*. Translated literally, it means "garden of children." In Germany on the first day of school, children are presented with paper cones filled with candy. Make your own cones out of patterned craft paper. (Scrapbook suppliers have a great variety of patterned and colored paper.) Roll a sheet of paper into a cone shape and staple the edges in place. Staple a ribbon or chenille stem across the top to create a handle. Fill the cones with pencils, stickers, and other small tokens for the children's first day visiting Germany.

Holidays and Celebrations

In Germany, it is considered bad luck to celebrate or wish someone a happy birthday before the actual day. So, just to be safe, a child may not get any birthday greetings or gifts until the day after her birthday. In addition to birthdays, Germans observe many holidays and celebrations throughout the year with their own special customs. Here are a few of the most popular celebrations:

Weihnachten (Christmas)

The Christmas season begins with the start of Advent. Children count down to Christmas one day at a time, often with the help of Advent calendars filled with chocolates. Christmas trees are traditionally lit with candles—not electric lights—and decorated with apples, nuts and candy, and blown-glass ornaments. St. Nicholas visits on December 6 and leaves goodies and presents in the children's shoes. Gingerbread and marzipan are popular holiday sweets. On Christmas Eve, the

children are summoned to the Christmas tree with a bell and the gifts are opened, followed by a feast and visit to church. Here are some ideas for celebrating your own German-style Christmas:

- Slice apples about 1/2" (13 mm) thick and brush with a lemon juice and water solution. Spread slices out on waxed paper to dry. Make a hole in the top of each apple slice for stringing. Turn the apples over every few days so that they dry completely on each side. Observe the changes in the apples as they dry. Thread ribbons through the dried apple slices and hang them along with other ornaments on your *Tannenbaum* tree.

- Have the children leave their shoes outside the classroom door on December 6 and have a parent come and fill the shoes with goodies. Or, leave a puzzle piece in each shoe, so that when the children put all of their pieces together, they complete a puzzle.

- Make an Advent calendar to count down the days until Christmas.

- Make copies of the Gingerbread House pattern **(page 60)** for the children. Have them decorate the candy houses with paint, sequins, or glitter.

Oktoberfest

Oktoberfest is a celebration of the harvest. Big parades with lavish floats and brass bands wind through the streets, while carnival rides, dancing, and sideshows fill the parks and side streets. Celebrate Oktoberfest by having the children create floats out of cardboard boxes. Have them choose themes and work in teams to decorate their floats with colored paper and crepe-paper streamers. Carry the floats while playing musical instruments as you parade throughout the school.

Erster Mai (May Day)

May Eve and May Day mark the time of year when Germans say good-bye to winter and hello to spring. On May Eve everyone makes as much noise as possible to chase away the evil winter spirits. Make soda can shakers to celebrate May Eve in the classroom. Spray paint empty aluminum soda cans. Have each child fill a can with a handful of dried beans. Cover the hole in the can with duct tape and decorate the outside of the can with gel pens, permanent markers, or other materials. Shake your noisemakers while engaging in May Eve revelry.

On May Day, a pole is created out of a tree that has been chopped down and stripped of its bark. This *Maibaum*, or Maypole, is erected in the town square and decorated with ribbons, garlands, and trinkets. Neighboring towns try to steal each other's Maypoles, so they must be guarded constantly. Divide the class into teams and give each team a large stick or dowel. Using an assortment of crepe-paper streamers, silk flowers, stickers, curling ribbon, and other collage materials, have each team decorate their Maypole. Plant the finished poles in the ground around the playground and make a game of conspiring to steal each other's Maypoles.

Martinstag (St. Martin's Day)

Children in Germany celebrate St. Martin's Day on November 11. On this day, children make or buy lanterns, which they carry through the streets while singing. The children go door-to-door and receive candy or other treats for their singing. Show your class how to make paper lanterns. Begin by coloring a sheet of 12" x 18" (30 cm x 46 cm) construction paper. Roll the paper so the short ends meet, and staple or glue the edges together. Punch two holes in the top of the lantern and

use to attach a 12" (30 cm) piece of string. Hang each lantern from a pole or stick. Pre-arrange with other teachers and staff at your school to have small treats to share with your class as you come to sing for them during your celebration of St. Martin's Day.

Famous Composers

Have you ever heard a lullaby by Brahms? Did you know that Bach had 13 children, many of whom became great composers themselves, or that Beethoven composed music even though he could not hear? Germany is the birthplace of many great classical composers still revered today. Long ago, many churches and government officials used to hire composers (people who write music) as full-time staff.

The following is a list of some famous German composers and some of their more famous works. Obtain a copy of each song and ask the children to lie on their backs with their eyes closed to listen to the music. Have the children vote for which music they like best.

> Johann Sebastian Bach (1685–1750) — *Brandenburg Concertos*
> Ludwig van Beethoven (1770–1827) — *Symphony no. 5 in C Minor*
> Johannes Brahms (1833–1897) — "Cradle Song"
> George Frideric Handel (1685–1759) — *Water Music*
> Richard Wagner (1813–1883) — "Ride of the Valkyries" from *The Valkyrie*

Grimms' Fairy Tales

The Grimm brothers, Jakob and Wilhelm, were storytellers who compiled many German folktales—stories that were passed orally from generation to generation—and wrote them into text. Some of their most famous tales include *Hansel and Gretel, Goldilocks and the Three Bears, The Frog King, Rapunzel, Rumpelstiltskin, Sleeping Beauty,* and *Snow White*.

Hold a fairy-tale festival where the class reads, discusses, and acts out a different story each day. Have the children rewrite the stories in their own words just like the brothers Grimm did. Encourage them to think of different endings for each of the stories as they write. Here are a few follow-up activities to go along with your study of the fairy tales listed above:

Hansel and Gretel

- Candy houses — Make copies of the Gingerbread House pattern (**page 60**) on heavy card stock. Have the children decorate their gingerbread houses by gluing on small candies with corn syrup.

- Bread-crumb trails — Have the children work in pairs to make trails for one another to follow using small scraps of paper. One child leaves a trail of scraps and the other child picks them up as he follows the path, then redistributes them along a new path.

Goldilocks and the Three Bears

- Porridge experiment — Make porridge (any hot breakfast cereal will do) and observe what happens to it as it changes from hot to cold.

- Museum of threes — Create a "museum of threes." Ask each child to find three objects at home or around the classroom that come in three graduated sizes, just like the things for Papa Bear, Mama Bear, and Baby Bear.

The Frog King

- Crowns — Make crowns fit for frogs (or kings) out of construction paper. Have the children decorate the crowns with jewels, sequins, and beads.

- Frog tales — Have each child draw and color a picture of a frog. Have the children bring pillows and pajamas to school. Set the frogs on the pillows and read them bedtime stories together as a class.

Rapunzel

- Wacky hair day — Ask the children to come to school sporting the most unique hairstyles they can imagine.

- Tug-of-war — Use Rapunzel's hair (a long rope) to see which half of the class can tug the other half of the class over a designated line marked on the floor.

Rumpelstiltskin

- Count gold — Toss a handful of pennies on the floor. Time each child for 10 seconds to see how many coins she can collect. Have the children examine and sort the coins to look for matching mint dates.

- Name search — Find out what each child's name means using a book of names or by searching on the Internet.

Sleeping Beauty

- Fairy wishes — Have the children write down three things they would wish for if they had a fairy to grant them wishes.

- Sleeping game — Have the children lie on their backs, pretending to be asleep. Choose one child to wake up a friend by placing a kiss (a chocolate candy kiss) on his forehead. The awakened prince or princess then finds a new friend to wake with a kiss.

Snow White

- Poison apple — Gather 10 apples that are similar in size and color. Place a small sticker on the bottom of one apple. Have the children work with partners: one child sorts and arranges the apples while the other hides his eyes. The second partner then tries to guess which apple has the hidden mark.

- Name the dwarfs — Ask the children to imagine that they are naming the seven dwarfs. What names would they use? Have each child draw a picture of seven dwarfs and give them all names.

Cuckoo Clock

8:00
9:00
10:00
11:00
12:00
1:00
2:00
3:00
4:00
5:00
6:00
7:00

59

Gingerbread House

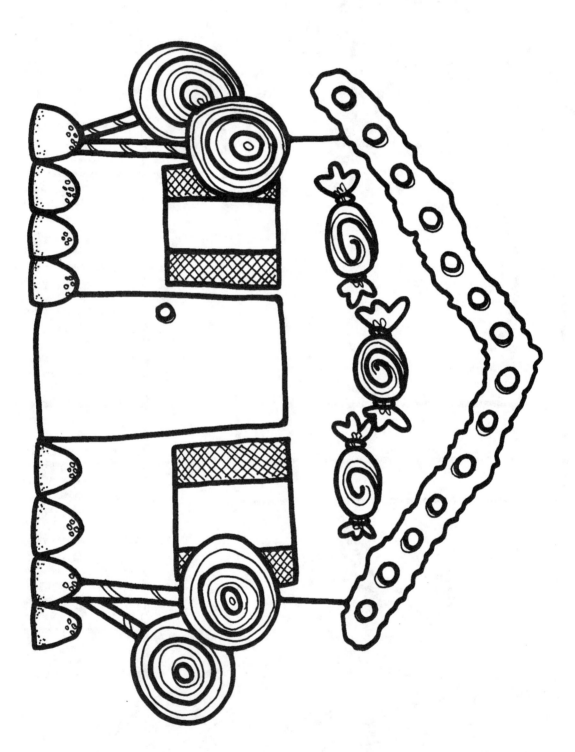

Children in Traditional German Dress

Flag of Germany

Directions: Color the stripes of the flag: black, red, and gold (top to bottom).

German Postcard, Globe Marker,
Luggage Sticker, and Passport Stamp

Postcard

Globe Marker

Luggage Sticker

Passport Stamp

India

Capital: New Delhi
Official Languages: Hindi, English

India is found in the southern part of Asia. It is the second most populous country in the world. Families in India work together on their farms. Even the children help with the farming.

In India, cows and monkeys are considered very special animals, so they are allowed to roam freely. It is not unusual to see a cow lying in the middle of a road undisturbed while cars and people navigate around it.

Get ready for an exciting journey to India! Here are a few Hindi words and phrases to help you get started:

English	Hindi
Hello / Good-bye	Namaste
Please	Kripyaa
Thank you	Dhanyavaad
You're welcome	Aapakaa svaagat hai
Yes	Ha
No	Nahi
1 – one	ek
2 – two	do
3 – three	teen
4 – four	chaar
5 – five	panch
6 – six	chai
7 – seven	saat
8 – eight	aath
9 – nine	nau
10 – ten	das

For more information about India:

Embassy of India
2107 Massachusetts Avenue NW
Washington, DC 20008

Phone: (202) 939-7000
Fax: (202) 265-4351
http://www.indianembassy.org/

Himalayan Climb

The world's highest mountains, the Himalayas, are found along India's border. Every year people flock from all over the world to scale these famous peaks. It is an extremely difficult climb, and it usually takes months to reach the summit. Talk with the children about things they have had to work hard to achieve. Maybe it was learning to ride a bike or writing a good story. Choose a challenging project or activity, such as reading 500 books, to complete as a class.

Draw a tall mountain shape on a bulletin board or sheet of poster board. On a separate sheet of paper draw a small person. Cut out the figure and tape it next to the bottom of the mountain. Make 100 marks going up the side of the mountain. For every book read by the class, move the person up one mark. When the climber reaches the summit, hold a celebration to mark the class's achievement.

Himalayan Hut

In the Indian countryside, homes are made out of wooden planks and palm tree leaves. Create Himalayan reading huts for your classroom by using large sheets of cardboard from appliance or furniture boxes. Attach or fold the cardboard sheets into three-sided huts. Stabilize the huts by attaching 2" (5 cm) strips of cardboard along the tops and bottoms of the open sides of the boxes. Cut several large palm fronds out of green craft paper. Lay the fronds across the tops of the huts and secure with tape. Place small pillows inside and allow the children to use their huts for reading and other quiet-time activities.

Tea and Spices

Tea and spices are big business in India. Farmers produce the spices and teas and export them all over the world. Select 10 different spices, such as cumin, mustard, chili powder, cinnamon, sage, or cloves. Place one teaspoon (5 mL) of each spice into two separate cups so that there are two cups of each spice. Cover the cups and poke a couple of holes in the tops. Mix up the cups and have the children try to match the spices by smell. Encourage them to talk about which spices they like best and why, or if certain spices remind them of certain times, people, or places.

Have the children create some spice doodles by first lightly drawing designs on paper with glue bottles. Choose spices of different colors. Have the children shake one spice over the paper at a time and then shake the paper to distribute the spice over the glue. Repeat with other spices.

Taj Mahal

The Taj Mahal is a famous structure built by Emperor Shah Jahan as a tribute to his wife. Its unique design and beautiful construction have made it one of the most famous buildings in the world. Using blocks or drawings, have the children create their own masterpieces of design and construction. Ask them to dedicate their works to loved ones.

Rubber

Rubber trees are an important crop in India. Rubber is made from the sap of these trees. As a class, make a list of things that are made out of rubber. Then create your own rubbery blob using the following recipe:

1 tbsp. (15 mL) white glue
1/2 tsp. (2.5 mL) borax powder
1/2 c. (120 mL) warm water

Combine the water and borax in a small cup and stir until well mixed. Place the glue in a second cup and add 1 tablespoon (15 mL) of the borax mixture. Stir with a spoon.

Have fun molding and playing with your rubbery blob. Try pressing a coin into it, or set it on the table and watch what happens. If you roll it into a ball, will it bounce? See how far you can stretch your blob before it breaks.

Pookalam

One popular art form in India is called *pookalam*. Pookalam is the art of arranging flowers into designs to create decorative floor mats. To make your own pookalam, give each child a sheet of craft paper cut into an 18" (46 cm) circle. Cut several smaller flower shapes out of colored construction paper. Encourage the children to use patterning techniques to create beautiful arrangements of flowers, gluing them onto their paper circles. Hang the finished pookalam creations on a bulletin board for the entire class to enjoy.

Chapati

Chapati is a flat bread and a common breakfast food in India. Make chapatis from the recipe below for a tasty breakfast treat.

1 3/4 c. (420 mL) whole wheat or chapati flour
3/4 c. (180 mL) water

Slowly add water to the flour and mix to form a soft dough. Knead the dough for at least five minutes until smooth. Cover the dough with a damp cloth and let sit for 20 minutes. Knead the dough again and divide it into 15 small balls. On a lightly floured surface, flatten the dough with a rolling pin until it is about 1/2" (13 mm) thick. Place the chapati in a frying pan, and fry it on each side for about one minute. Spread jam or honey on top.

Melas and Bazars

In India you can often find a *mela* or *bazar* in progress. A mela is a fair that can include puppet shows, circus acts, magicians, livestock races, plays, singing, and dancing. A bazar also has crafts, textiles, and food for sale. Hold a combined mela and bazar in your classroom. Let the children

choose what they will present at the mela. Will they put on a puppet show, or will they make a small craft to sell? Work with each child individually (or in teams) to make a plan for their part in the mela /bazar. Spend time each day making preparations for the event. Have the children make signs to announce what their booths or activites include. On the final day of the week, hold your mela /bazar and have the children take turns visiting one another in their booths. Invite other classes to visit and enjoy the food and entertainment.

Monsoons

India has two monsoon seasons. During monsoon season, it rains every day. Often the rains turn to floods if too much rain falls too quickly. Some parts of India receive around 125" (318 mm) of rain during monsoon season. How much does it rain where you live? Obtain a rain gauge from a local hardware or general merchandise store. Place the gauge outside where it can be seen through a classroom window without being disturbed.

Keep a class graph of the total rainfall for your area for one month. Draw a 1" (25 mm) grid with 30–31 columns (depending on the number of days in the month) and 10–12 rows. Have the children take turns checking the rain gauge and marking the graph with the total number of inches of rain received. If you receive only 1/2 " (13 mm) of rain the first day, color in half of the first box on your graph. After a month has passed, use the data from the graph to answer questions: Which day received the most rain? Which day had the least? Did the rain all seem to come at once, or was it spread out evenly throughout the month? Encourage the children to consider what might happen if they had as much rain as during monsoon season in India.

Diwali (Festival of Lights)

Diwali is a five-day Hindu celebration marking the end of the monsoon season and the beginning of the harvest. It celebrates the triumph of good over evil, light over darkness. The date of Diwali is based on the lunar calendar (when moon phases occur), but it generally falls in October or November on the night of a new moon. During Diwali homes are lit with lamps and other lights to welcome Lakshmi, goddess of wealth and prosperity. People clean and decorate their homes, purchase new clothes, and prepare feasts. Each evening there are fireworks to enjoy.

Spend a day preparing for a Diwali celebration. Have the children help you clean and decorate the room using the colors of the Indian flag: orange, white, and green. Make a copy of the Diawali Candles pattern **(page 69)** for each child. Have the children write their wishes for good fortune on the candles, and line the room with the candle wishes.

Extend the candle activity by making several copies of the Diwali Candles pattern on colored paper. Cut out the candles and laminate them. Using a dry-erase or washable marker, divide the bottom half of your classroom windows into 12" (30 cm) boxes. In each box write a numeral (e.g., 6) or a math sentence (e.g., 2 + 4 =). Have the children model the numeral or complete the math sentences by taping the appropriate number of candles in each box. Let the children remove the candles and erase the problem, and then start again by writing their own numerals and number sentences. The children's candles in the windows will add a nice decorative touch to the classroom.

Tag Games

One of India's national pastimes is a game called *kabaddi*. Kabaddi is similar to a game of tag except the person who is "It" must hold his breath until he tags someone. While in a real game of kabaddi a person gets tagged by tackling, you can use the more gentle method of tagging by touch. Divide the class into two teams and designate two separate territories. Choose one child to be "It" first. That child must hold her breath as she crosses the line and tries to tag people on the opposing team. Those who are trying not to get tagged must repeat "kabaddi" over and over.

Five Shells

Five shells is a popular game among Indian children. It is a great game to exercise fine motor skills and to practice counting. Have three or four players sit in a circle. The first player places five small shells, about 1" (25 mm) in diameter, in a pile in the middle of the circle. The player tries to pick up one shell from the pile without disturbing any of the other shells. If he is successful, he must toss the shell in the air and grab a second shell from the pile before catching the first. If he disturbs the other shells, the next player takes a turn. With practice, all five shells can be picked up in one turn.

Mehndi

On special days, children in India paint designs on their hands with henna, a reddish brown dye made from plants. This practice is called *Mehndi*. Have the children trace their hands on sheets of paper. Using markers or rubber stamps, have them color or decorate their paper hands with ornate designs and patterns.

Rangoli

Rangoli is a traditional Indian art of floor painting. People typically paint the thresholds of their homes with simple geometric shapes or with images that tell a story. In some parts of India, these floor paintings are created at dawn and dusk every single day. Each day you visit India, have the children begin the day by creating a rangoli, decorating a 24" (61 cm) square sheet of craft paper with sidewalk chalk or markers. Tape the finished rangoli designs on the floor around the classroom. By the end of the week, your floor may be completely covered with these interesting decorations.

Bell Dancing

Dancers from India tell stories with their hands and tie bells around their feet to jingle with every step. Show the children how to string jingle bells on ribbons or chenille stems. Then have them twist or tie the bells around their ankles and dance to a selection of Indian music. "India Blue" from Ali Akbar Khan's *Garden of Dreams* album (Triloka, 2002) would be a nice choice.

Indian Folklore

Check out a book of Indian myths or folklore, such as *One Grain of Rice* by Demi (Scholastic, 1997) or *The Rumor* by Jan Thornhill (Maple Tree Press, 2005), and share stories of Indian culture with your class.

Diwali Candles

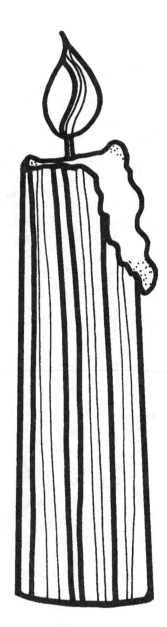

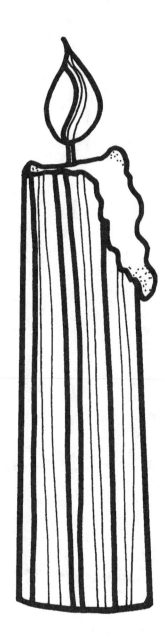

Children in Traditional Indian Dress

Flag of India

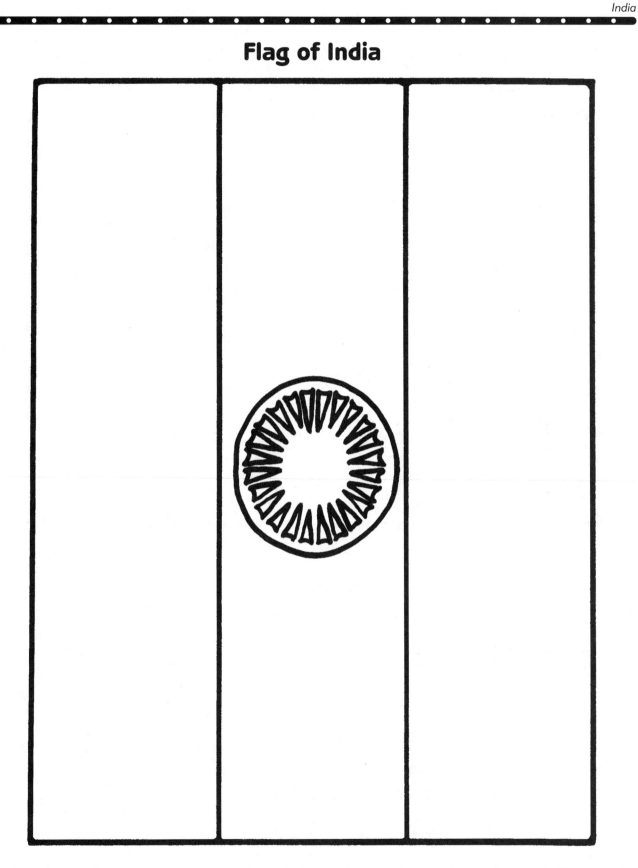

Directions: Color the stripes on the flag: orange, white, and green (top to bottom). The wheel is black.

Indian Postcard, Globe Marker,
Luggage Sticker, and Passport Stamp

The Taj Mahal...

Postcard

Luggage Sticker

India

Globe Marker

Passport Stamp

India

India

Iran

Capital: Tehran
Official Language: Persian (Farsi)

Iran is an oil-rich country located in southern Asia along the Persian Gulf. Children in Iran live in many different kinds of homes. In the cities, they live in high-rise apartments and homes with flat roofs. These roofs are ideal places to relax and entertain. Children who live on farms dwell in small houses surrounded by farmland. Still others, called nomads, roam the countryside stopping only where there is good grazing ground for their animals. A child living a nomadic lifestyle typically lives in a tent.

Regardless of where you live, you will enjoy getting to know more about the country of Iran. Here are a few Persian (also called Farsi) words and phrases to help you get started:

English	Persian (Farsi)
Hello	Sa'lam
Good-bye	Kho'da ha'fez
Please	Kh'hesh mi'ko'nam
Thank you	Mo'teh'shaker'am
Yes	Ba'leh
No	Nah
1 – one	yek
2 – two	dow
3 – three	seh
4 – four	cha'har
5 – five	pang
6 – six	shesh
7 – seven	haft
8 – eight	hasht
9 – nine	noh
10 – ten	dah

For more information about Iran:

Embassy of Pakistan
Interests Section of the Islamic Republic of Iran
2209 Wisconsin Avenue NW
Washington, DC 20007

Phone: (202) 965-4990
Fax: (202) 965-1073
http://www.daftar.org/Eng/default
.asp?lang=eng

Changes for Iran

Iran's history is marked by change. Even its own name has changed: the country used to be called Persia until the Shah, leader of Iran, changed the name officially to Iran.

In the 1900s oil was discovered in Iran. This brought immediate opportunities for export and economic growth. Many new ideas were introduced to Iran through trade with the Western world. A new government, however, soon restricted these interests. Western influences such as movie theaters and universities were soon closed, and women were once again required to wear head coverings. When you see an Iranian woman in public today, you will see her wearing a piece of cloth that covers her head and shoulders.

Discuss the children's opinions about these changes and how they think the people of Iran might have felt. If they were to rename their own state or country, what name would they choose? Have the children consider some of the changes that have occurred in their own lives. Perhaps they have a new parent or sibling, have moved to a new home, or experienced a death of a loved one. Have the children choose one event and write about the impact it has had on their lives. Ask them to illustrate their ideas and then share their thoughts with the rest of the class.

Oil

Oil is still one of Iran's major exports. Since it would be impractical to use crude oil in your classroom, have fun with these oil-based activities using vegetable oil:

- They say that oil and water do not mix, but is that really true? Find out by filling a water bottle half full of water colored with food coloring. Fill the rest of the bottle with oil. Securely tighten the lid and shake the bottle gently. Watch as the water and oil separate. Now shake the bottle as hard as you can so that the oil and water are thoroughly mixed. Have the children check back on the experiment in 5, 10, and 30 minutes. How long does it take for the water and oil to separate?

- Fill a disposable pan with 1/4" (7 mm) of water. Pour a large tablespoon of oil-based paint in the water. Draw a toothpick or a plastic knife through the paint until it swirls and swoops in the water. Add other colors of paint if desired. Press a sheet of heavy card stock onto the top of the water and gently remove it. Turn the paper over to reveal your marbleized paper art.

- Gather several different varieties of oil, such as olive, sesame, peanut, vegetable, and canola. Place one drop of each along the edge of a flat baking pan. Tell the class that you are having oil races. Have them guess which oil is the most viscous (thick) and will take the longest to run to the other edge of the pan. After creating a graph of the children's predictions, carefully raise the side of the pan until the oil drops begin to flow. Watch for the first and last oils to reach the other side of the pan.

Salty Landforms

Iran borders on the Caspian Sea. The Volga and Ural rivers flow into the sea, but there is no way out for the water. This creates a very salty sea. Two interesting phenomena occur as a result: everything floats in the salty water; and, as the water evaporates, a salty residue is left behind.

The Dasht-e Kavir is a desert in Iran that is harsh and uninhabitable. Although it seldom rains, the water from rain and the sandy soil combine to create a salty crust on the desert floor.

Here are several ideas to help you explore some of the properties of salt:

- To demonstrate how salt water makes things float, have the children fill a clear glass with water. Add an egg or other sinking object to the water. Slowly add table salt, stirring gently one spoonful at a time, until the egg rises to the top and floats. Explain that the change in the density of the water makes the egg float.

- Remove the egg and pour some of the salt water into the bottom of a foil pan. Place the pan in a sunny window to encourage rapid evaporation. Check back in a day or two to see what is left once when the water evaporates.

- Take a chenille stem and twist it into a spiral. Fill a cup with hot water and add several spoonfuls of salt to the water until no more salt can be added. Stick the chenille stem into the cup and allow the solution to sit undisturbed for several days. Remove the chenille stem and observe the salt crystals that have formed.

- Cover a sheet of paper completely by painting it with watercolor paint. Take a sponge brush and reapply water over the entire surface of the painting. Using a saltshaker, shake salt over the picture. Watch the painting transform as the salt dissolves into the water on the paper.

- Gather several different varieties of salt, including table salt, kosher salt, pickling salt, sea salt, and Epsom salts. Pour a small spoonful of each salt on a plate and have the children use magnifying glasses to examine the salt varieties for similarities and differences.

- Fill two plastic, zippered sandwich bags, one with salt and the other with sugar. Label the bags A and B. Ask the children to guess which bag contains salt and which contains sugar. Tell the children that they can discover which one is which without tasting the contents. Take a small amount from each bag and make two little piles in a foil pan. Using a lit candle, put the flame close to each substance. The sugar will heat and begin to burn, but the salt will not.

Calligraphy

Calligraphy, or the art of decorative lettering, is practiced widely throughout Iran. Share some calligraphic writing samples in Farsi (good sources are available on the Internet) with the class. Point out that another interesting fact about the writing is that it is written from right to left.

Pass out sheets of lined paper and encourage the children to try writing their names from right to left. If possible, supply calligraphic markers for this activity. Next, encourage the children to write a few sentences, starting with the first word on the right-hand side of the page and working across toward the left. If the children seem discouraged, remind them that children from Iran would probably find it just as difficult trying to write from left to right.

Halvah

There are many different recipes for making Halvah, a sweet Iranian treat. Here is a simple one to try in your classroom:

1 c. (240 mL) sesame seeds
2 tbsp. (30 mL) honey
1 tsp. (5 mL) vanilla extract
1 tsbp. (15 mL) cocoa or carob powder

Grind the sesame seeds to create a nut butter. Scrape the seeds into a bowl and drizzle the honey on top. Mix well until the seeds and honey form a sticky mass. Stir in the vanilla and cocoa powder, and mix well (the mixture will look marbled). Press the mixture into the bottom of the plastic container lined with waxed paper. Refrigerate for about one hour. Remove and cut into cubes. (Recipe source: http://www.recipegoldmine.com.)

Polo

Polo is a game that was invented in Iran. Players ride ponies on a field and try to score points by hitting a ball through a goal using mallets. It is a very competitive and fast-paced game, and one you will enjoy adapting for your classroom.

First, everyone will need a pony. Use the Polo Pony pattern **(pages 78–79)** to make the two sides of the pony's head. Make one copy of both pages for each child. Let the children color their ponies, then cut them out. Staple the two patterns together (colored sides facing out), leaving the bottom open, and attach to a wooden dowel or yardstick/meterstick. Decorate the finished ponies by adding ribbons, yarn, or other embellishments to the manes.

Create mallets out of wooden dowels and plastic soda bottles. Carefully carve an "X" into the side of each empty one-liter soda bottle with a craft knife. Then press a wooden dowel into the bottle and secure in place with colored duct tape or electrical tape. More mallet decorations may be made with stickers, colored tape, or gel markers.

Mark off a large rectangular area for the polo field. Mark a goal at each end of the field by placing two cones about 6' (1.83 m) apart. Have four children play at a time. Players must stay on their ponies at all times. Mallets may only be used to hit the ball—not other ponies or players. The object of the game is to hit the ball through the opponent's goal, using the sides of the mallets (not ends, as in croquet) to strike the ball. A polo club match typically consists of four or six 7-minute time periods called chukkas. Select the appropriate number of chukkas for the time allowed and interest of your class.

No Ruz

Ela-eh Shoma Mobarak! Happy New Year! No Ruz is the Iranian celebration of the beginning of spring. The No Ruz celebration lasts for 13 days. Before the celebration, homes are cleaned and new clothes are purchased to welcome in the New Year. Barley, wheat, or lentils are sprouted, and many sweet breads and other foods are prepared in anticipation of the celebration.

During the first few days of No Ruz, families spend time visiting relatives, exchanging gifts, and feasting on good food. On the 13th and final day of No Ruz, families leave their homes to spend the day enjoying nature and the new growth of spring.

One No Ruz tradition involves setting out seven items on the table: wheat or barley, fish, lit candles, mirrors, wine or vinegar, eggs, and garlic. Each of the seven items symbolizes a different aspect of spring, such as new growth or abundance. All seven items also start with the letter "s" in Persian (Farsi).

Here are some activities to include in your own No Ruz celebration:

- Spend one day cleaning out the classroom, desks, lockers, or cubbies in preparation for the New Year.

- Invite each child to bring one small object from home to give away in a class gift exchange.

- See how many things in the classroom you can group into sets of 13—e.g., 13 blue markers, 13 paper clips, etc.

- Fill three small foil pans with damp potting soil. Soak barley, wheat, and lentils overnight and then plant them in the soil pans—each variety in its own pan. Water and place the pans in a sunny window to germinate. Observe and record the changes in each plant. Ask the children to guess which pan will sprout first. Continue to watch the sprouts grow over the next few weeks.

- Have each child bring in seven items (or pictures of items cut from magazines or newspapers) that begin with the letter "s." Make a No Ruz word bank by listing all of the items that the children bring.

- Plan a day at the park in celebration of spring. Enjoy the flora and fauna of the area you are visiting. Ask the children to look for signs of spring or of new growth and life. Encourage them to look at the park from new perspectives—looking up, down, behind, or under—and see if they discover something new. Have the children write a journal page about their visit to the park, describing what they saw, heard, smelled, felt, and tasted while they were there.

Goat Herd

Many Iranian children who live in the country help their families by tending sheep or goats. Make several copies of the Goat Herd pattern **(page 80)**. Laminate and cut out the cards. Make a second set of cards on colorful paper. Write the numbers 1–20 or different math sentences on this set of cards.

The object of the game is to get all the goats from one end of the pasture into the pen for the night. Spread the plain goat cards out on the left-hand side of the table. Place two box lids on the right for goat pens. Stack the numbered cards facedown on the table. Have the children play with partners, taking turns turning over the top card. Each player moves the number of goats indicated on the card into his pen. Play continues until all of the goats are safely home. Count to see how many goats each player collected.

Polo Pony (1)

Polo Pony (2)

Goat Herd

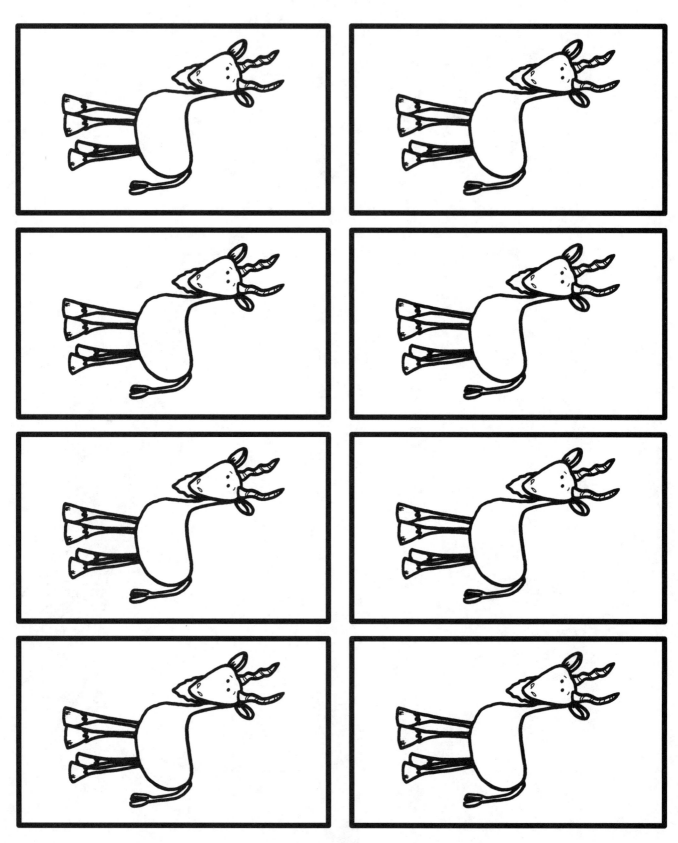

Children in Traditional Iranian Dress

Flag of Iran

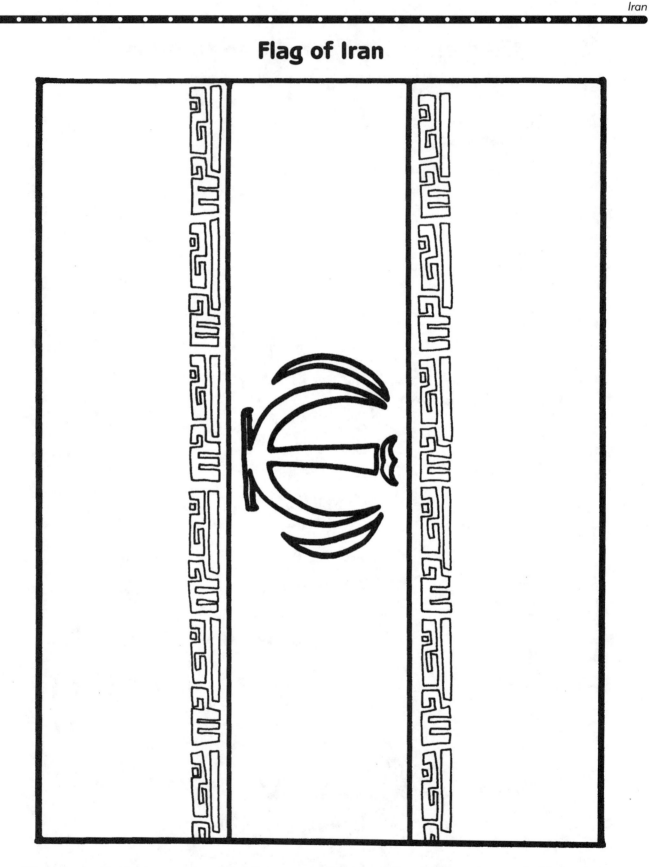

Directions: Color the stripes of the flag: green, white, and red (top to bottom). Make the emblem red.

Iranian Postcard, Globe Marker,
Luggage Sticker, and Passport Stamp

Postcard

Globe Marker

Luggage Sticker

Passport Stamp

Italy

Capital: Rome
Official Language: Italian

Italy is found in the southern part of Europe. It is a peninsula surrounded by seas. One interesting fact about Italy is that there is another country situated completely within its borders. Vatican City is considered a separate country-state. It has its own government and currency, but it is located entirely inside the country of Italy.

As you learn the words and phrases below, notice the similarities with Portuguese and Spanish. All three are Romance languages.

English	Italian
Hello/good-bye	Ciao
Good morning	Buongiorno
Thank you	Grazie
Please	Per favore
Yes	Sì
No	No
1 – one	uno
2 – two	due
3 – three	tre
4 – four	quattro
5 – five	cinque
6 – six	sei
7 – seven	sette
8 – eight	otto
9 – nine	nove
10 – ten	dieci

For more information about Italy:

Embassy of Italy
3000 Whitehaven Street NW
Washington, DC 20008

Phone: (202) 612-4400
Fax: (202) 518-2154
http://www.italyemb.org/

Concrete Creations

The Romans are credited with inventing concrete. This useful building material is the foundation for strong roads and buildings. In Italy, you can see it in ancient Roman structures like the Pantheon and some aqueducts. Create your own concrete garden path to celebrate your visit to Italy. Mix quick-set concrete according to the package directions. Pour the concrete into foil cake pans and let it set for 5 to 10 minutes. Have the children gently press their hands into the concrete to make impressions and then wash their hands thoroughly with soapy water. Provide shells, rocks, or other interesting stones for the children to press into the concrete around the edges of the pans. Using sticks or sharp pencils, have the children scratch their names and the date into their stepping stones. Let the stepping stones harden completely overnight and remove the foil pans. Use the stones to line a garden walkway, or send them home as parent gifts.

An interesting fact about making concrete is that it will actually cure or harden underwater. To experiment with this concept, create some plaster of paris (which has some of the same properties as concrete, but is not as strong) by mixing according to the package directions. Ask the children to predict or hypothesize about what will happen if they pour water into the cups of plaster. Fill plastic cups 1/2 full of the mixed plaster. Then fill the rest of the cups with water. Let the children place their hands around the cups. Most likely they will be able to detect heat. This is due to the chemical change occurring inside the cups. After a few minutes, you should see that the plaster has set (or cured) even though it was sitting in water.

Frescoes

Michelangelo (1475–1564) was a famous Renaissance artist who often painted frescoes. Frescoes are paintings that are made right in the wet plaster of walls or ceilings. One of Michelangelo's most famous frescoes was painted on the roof of the Sistine Chapel in the Vatican. It took the artist four years (most of it lying on his back) to complete the masterpiece.

To create your own frescoes, mix plaster of paris as instructed on the package directions. Pour the plaster 3/8" (10 mm) deep into foil cake pans. As the mixture begins to harden, create a small hole in each pan of plaster with the end of a paintbrush or pencil. Have the children use watercolor paints to create their own fresco paintings. Allow the plaster to cure overnight. Remove the pans and paint the reverse sides too, if desired. Thread ribbons through the holes so the frescoes can be hung on the wall.

Mosaics

Mosaics are another art form for which Italians are well-known. While mosaics are typically created in tile, you can easily create your own using 1" (25 mm) squares of colorful construction paper. Have the children glue the colored squares onto sheets of art paper so that all of the colors touch. Encourage them to arrange the squares to create unique patterns or pictures.

Volcanoes

Italy has two very famous active volcanoes: Mount Etna and Stromboli. Create your own volcano in class by burying an empty tin can in the middle of a pile of damp sand. Mold the sand up and around the sides of the can to create a volcano shape. Mix a few drops of red food coloring and liquid dish soap with 1/2 (120 mL) cup of vinegar and 2 cups (470 mL) of water. Carefully

spoon 2 tablespoons (30 mL) of baking soda into the can inside the volcano. Then gently pour a little of the liquid into the can and watch the lava flow. Substitute different powdered substances (e.g., baking powder, cornstarch, etc.) or change the ratio of vinegar and water, and try your volcano experiment again.

Leaning Tower of Pisa

The town of Pisa has a bell tower that is leaning. It is leaning so far that the bells can no longer ring. Several people have studied the tower and have suggested ways to keep it from sinking further or falling over. See how high the children can build a tower of wooden blocks. Count the number of blocks in each tower and rebuild the towers trying to build them higher each time. Have the tower builders ring a bell to celebrate their new construction heights.

Venice

Venice is a famous city in Italy built on several tiny islands. Over 400 bridges link the islands that are separated by canals. If you do not want to use the bridges, a gondolier will row you through the canals in a gondola, a narrow, flat-bottomed boat that has a high peak on each end.

Build your own bridges over the canals in Venice. Cut several island shapes out of craft paper. Tape the island shapes randomly on the classroom floor. Number the islands 1–20 or using multiples of 2, 5, or 10. You could also take pairs of islands and write a math sentence on one and the solution on the other. Have the children build bridges of yarn between the islands. If the islands are numbered sequentially, have the children connect the islands in order, measuring the distance from one to the next and cutting lengths of yarn to fit. If you are using math sentences, have the children build bridges between the equations and the answers.

Pasta

While in Venice, stop at a small bistro and enjoy your favorite pasta as a snack. Have the children examine some pasta before cooking and then again after you have boiled it according to the package directions. Once the pasta has been cooked and drained, toss it with some olive oil or butter and some garlic or Parmesan cheese.

Extend the activity by making graphs, mosaics, or other projects with an assortment of uncooked pasta.

If you need a break during your Italian celebration, play this fun stretching game. Large, ring-shaped pasta with a meat or cheese filling is called *tortelloni*. The same pasta in a smaller size is called *tortellini*. Tell the class that when you say "tortelloni," they should stand up tall. When you say "tortellini," they should scrunch down as small as possible. Alternate saying "tortelloni" and "tortellini" to work out the wiggles.

Roman Coliseum

A coliseum is a large arena used for playing sports. The English language gets this word from the Colosseum in Rome. The Colosseum was a large arena for gladiators and other sports and entertainment hundreds of years ago. Part of this mighty structure still stands today.

Mark off an area in your classroom or on the playground to create your own coliseum. Plan a gladiator contest, such as "Last One Standing," to take place in the arena. To play, send two children to the center of the coliseum as gladiators. Ask them to shake hands and wish each other good luck. Challenge the children to perform a feat, such as standing on one leg while holding the other behind their backs. In this case, the gladiators must stay on one foot during the contest. The last one still standing on one foot wins. Gladiators can gently chase or bump into one another to try to knock each other off balance. Add three or more gladiators to the coliseum for added action.

Italian Gelato

Italians are credited with inventing ice cream. Gelato is soft, rich ice cream served everywhere in Italy. Use the Italian Gelato pattern **(page 89)** to build words from your spelling or vocabulary lists. Make several copies of the page on colorful paper. Cut out all of the ice-cream scoops and place them in a large bin. Ask the children to create ice-cream words by writing a word on a cone, then adding one scoop of ice cream for each letter in the word. Have the children glue the cones onto 12" x 18" (30 cm x 46 cm) sheets of construction paper, then add the lettered scoops in order on top.

Extend this activity by creating file folder games with the ice-cream patterns. Make several copies of the Italian Gelato page on colorful paper. Glue six cones on each side of the file folder. Write a different word or math sentence on each cone. Then write rhyming words or answers to the math sentences on the scoops of ice cream. Laminate the scoops and the file folder separately. Have the children use tape or other adhesive to stack the scoops on the appropriate cones.

Build a Pizza

Pizza is another popular culinary contribution of the Italians. Make several copies of the Build a Pizza pattern **(page 90)**. Make four crusts by cutting 8" (20 cm) circles out of tan or ivory paper. Color and cut out the pizza toppings and then laminate all of the pieces. Place each pizza topping in a separate bag. To play the game, give each player a crust. One player rolls a die. That player chooses a topping and then adds the same number of pieces as shown on the die. For example, if she rolls a five, the child may add five of any topping to her pizza. Play continues until all of the toppings have been used. At that point, reverse the game, having the children remove the same number of toppings as shown on the die. The first one to completely remove all toppings from his pizza gets to start the next game.

Use the pizza patterns for activities exploring fractions, too. Make copies of the pizza pattern page and color the toppings. Glue the toppings onto the crusts as desired. Leave one pizza whole, cut another in half, and cut the others into thirds and fourths. Laminate the pizza pieces. Use them to demonstrate fractions and for various math activities. Extend the activity by cutting up a real pizza and then eating the fractions together as a class.

You can also use the pizza patterns as a kind of incentive chart. Create individual pizzas as described above. Cut each pizza into eight slices. Mount empty pizza boxes (or other flat boxes) to a bulletin board and write each child's name on a box. Set a goal for behavior or learning (such as walking in the hall quietly or learning fact families), and then let the children earn slices to their pizzas as they accomplish their goals. Attach the slices inside the pizza boxes as they are earned, and have a pizza party when everyone has completed their pizzas.

Rossini

Gioacchino Rossini (1792–1868) is a famous composer from Italy. Many of his works are widely recognized, such as the "William Tell Overture" and *The Barber of Seville*. Rossini is best known for his operas. Obtain a copy of some of his compositions and play them for the class. Have the children dance or draw to the music, or act out what they think is happening in the story. Discuss what the children liked about the music as well as what they did not like. Have them imagine what life would have been like as a composer.

Using colored handbells or a xylophone, have the children compose and play their own music. Create a music staff by drawing five horizontal lines on a piece of paper. Make a copy for each child. Cut 1/2" (13 mm) circles out of colored paper to match the colors of the bells or bars on the xylophone. Have the children glue the circles on their music staffs in any order. Then have them play the pieces they have composed by ringing the bell or tapping the bar that matches the color of each dot on their music staffs.

Mona Lisa

Leonardo da Vinci (1452–1519) is a famous Italian painter and scientist. One of his most famous pieces is the *Mona Lisa*. Obtain a print or copy of the *Mona Lisa* to share with the class. Talk about the woman's intriguing smile and what she might tell the children if the painting could talk. Have the children paint portraits of their own on paper, then write stories about the people they have painted.

Galileo

Galileo (1564–1642) is another famous Italian. He was a scientist that studied planets, stars, and space. During his explorations, Galileo invented the telescope and discovered that Earth and the other planets orbit the sun. Up until this time, people thought that Earth was the center of the universe and that everything else revolved around it. Galileo's discoveries were not very popular at the time.

On the Runway

Italy is known as the fashion and design capital of the world. Many people who design clothing and furniture study the trends and fashions that are created in Italy. Have the children bring one interesting piece of clothing from home to wear in a class fashion show. It may be a special shirt purchased on a vacation, a gift from someone special, or a costume, or some clothing purchased for a special occasion. Have each child describe why the article of clothing is special on a piece of paper. Read the children's descriptions as they parade individually across the front of the classroom.

Italian Gelato

Build a Pizza

Children in Traditional Italian Dress

Flag of Italy

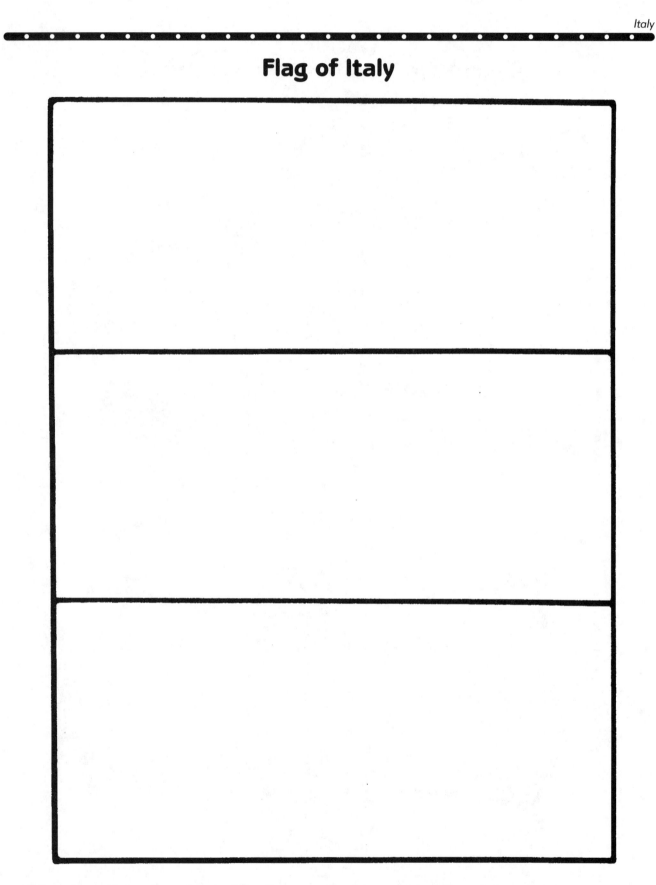

Directions: Color the strirpes of the flag: green, white, and red (from left to right).

Italian Postcard, Globe Marker,
Luggage Sticker, and Passport Stamp

Postcard

Globe
Marker

Luggage
Sticker

Passport
Stamp

Jamaica

Capital: Kingston

Official Language: English (Jamaican Patois also spoken)

Jamaica is an island in the Caribbean, just south of Cuba. With its beautiful beaches, Jamaica is a popular tourist destination. It was first settled by the Arawak Indians. They called the island Xaymaca, which means "Land of woods and water." Jamaica used to be a colony of England, but the people successfully fought for independence in the late 20th century. Many of the people who live in Jamaica are descendants of African slaves. There is a colorful mixture of cultures and people who now call Jamaica home.

Most Jamaicans speak some form of English. Some use proper English, while others speak Jamaican Patois, which is a blending of English and African. Even if you don't speak Patois, you can probably figure out what is being said because it is very close to English. Here are some words and phrases that you might hear someone from Jamaica use:

English	Jamaican Patois
Brother	Bredda
Breakfast	Brekfus
Child	Chile
Daughter	Dawta
Is	Deh
For	Fah
Rude	Faisty
Mosquito	Maskita
Me, I	Mi
Only	Ongle
Something	Sinting
Good-bye	Wakgud

Source: *Jamaica* (Cultures of the World) by Sean Sheehan and Angela Black. Times Media, 1996.

For more information about Jamaica:

Embassy of Jamaica
1520 New Hampshire Avenue NW
Washington, DC 20036

Phone: (202) 452-0660
Fax: (202) 452-0081

School Uniforms

For many years in Jamaica, only children of families who could afford to send children to private schools attended school. The Jamaican government has since worked hard to provide access to school for all children.

Jamaican children typically wear uniforms to school. Boys wear cotton pants and shirts (usually tan), and girls wear blue jumpers with white shirts. You may have school uniforms at your school, too. Talk with the class about whether they think school uniforms are a good idea or not. Then give each child a sheet of paper. Ask the children to imagine that they are in charge of creating new school uniforms. Have the children generate their own designs, including illustrations as well as descriptions of the new clothes. Hang all of the illustrations on a wall for the entire class to see.

Recycled Toys

Since many of the children in Jamaica are not wealthy, they have become very resourceful. They will make toys out of just about anything. A pile of rags can be wound and tied to make a soccer ball. An old tire rim and a stick make for fun rolling and tossing with a friend. Even juice boxes are stuffed with paper and pressed into round shapes to make balls for play. Provide an assortment of recyclable items such as newspapers, rags, tin cans, and boxes, and encourage the children to create their own unique toys.

Make a ball out of rags or a container stuffed with newspaper to play a variation of a game called "Dandy Shandy". Have the children stand in a circle. Ask two or three volunteers to stand in the middle of the circle. The children in the circle take turns rolling or tossing the ball underhand, trying to tag the feet or legs of the children in the middle. Those who are in the middle may dodge the ball in any way they choose. The children will enjoy watching each other's acrobatic gyrations as they try to avoid being hit by the ball.

Bauxite

Bauxite is a mineral that is mined in Jamaica. It is used to make aluminum. Aluminum is a lightweight metal. Try these fun activities to explore aluminum in the classroom:

- Gather a large assortment of aluminum cans to make noisemakers. Wash thoroughly and spray paint a variety of colors. Punch a hole in the bottom of each can with an awl or nail. Have the children decorate the cans with gel markers, stickers, or other objects. Insert strings into the cans and tape securely in place. Tie two or three cans together. Hold the cans by the strings and shake them up and down to make clanging music.

- Paint an aluminum can a bright color and use it as a ball in a game of soccer. Have the children see if they can kick the can from one end of the playing field to the other.

- Give each child a 24" (61 cm) sheet of aluminum foil. Have them fold their sheets in half lengthwise, trying to make as few wrinkles as possible. Then show them how to accordion-fold the folded strips into 4" (10 cm) sections. Have the children draw a picture and write a description of their illustration for each section on one side of the folded strip. Provide pencils, gel pens, or permanent markers. Refold the foil strips accordion-style and staple along the folded edges to create little foil books.

Cricket

Cricket is a popular sport in Jamaica. The game is played with two teams, and official matches can last for days. Try these simplified rules to play a game of "Almost-Cricket":

Designate a playing field and place two cones or markers about 20 feet (6 m) apart in the middle. These cones, called "wickets," mark where the runners run. Cricket players normally use a special bat that is flat on one side and rounded on the other. To make things simple, players in this game of Almost-Cricket can simply throw or kick the ball. Divide the class into two teams. One team spreads out in the field around the cones. The other team is up to bat. Two of the players from the batting team line up, one at the first cone and the other at the second. The other players wait off to the side for their turn to bat.

The bowler (pitcher) stands next to one of the wickets (cones) and bowls the ball by bouncing it toward the player at the other wicket. The ball should bounce once before reaching the batter. The player at bat kicks or catches and throws the ball (preferably away from a player who is in the field) and then runs to the other wicket. Her teammate runs to the first wicket at the same time, so they trade places. Players can continue to run between the wickets as long as they are safe from getting tagged by the other team with the ball. Each time the runners switch, they score a point. The bowler "pitches" to the other runner for the second pitch from the wicket opposite where the player is standing. After 6 runs, the runners exchange places with the next two players on their team. After 3 "outs" or 12 runs, the teams trade places so that the team that was batting is now in the field and the fielders are now batting.

To put a runner out, players can catch a thrown or kicked ball, or they may tag the runner with the ball when he is between wickets.

Reggae Music

Bob Marley is a famous musician who pioneered the reggae music movement in Jamaica. Gather a selection of Bob Marley's albums, such as *One Love* or *Legend*, to play in the classroom. Have the children make musical instruments out of tin cans, boxes, yogurt containers, and other recyclable materials. Encourage the children to play their musical instruments while dancing and moving to the reggae music.

Anansi

Many years ago, the African slaves who were brought to Jamaica to work in the sugar-cane fields were not allowed to participate in any of their own cultural practices. That meant no singing and no dancing. The only way the Africans could pass on their heritage to their children was through bedtime stories. Many of the stories handed down from generation to generation are stories of Anansi, a mischievous and crafty spider.

There are many tales of the exploits of Anansi the spider. Find a collection from the library (look under the subject of Jamaican folklore) and share the stories with the children during reading time. After sharing the tales, encourage the children to write and illustrate their own stories about the crafty spider.

Make models of Anansi the spider with the children. Paint 4" (10 cm) Styrofoam balls with thinned glue or liquid starch. Cover the wet glue with small strips of black tissue paper to make the spider bodies. Allow the glue to dry completely. Make a copy of the Anansi the Spider pattern **(page 98)** for each child. Have the children color the head and legs of Anansi as desired. Glue or tape toothpicks to the backs of the legs so that at least 1" (25 mm) of each toothpick extends beyond the top. Stick the legs into the Styrofoam ball and then glue Anansi's head onto the body. Hang each Anansi from the ceiling with a piece of string. Attach a second piece of string tied to a paper clip to the bottom of the spider. Hang the children's stories and artwork from the bottoms of their spiders.

Jamaican Juice

There are many kinds of fruits grown in Jamaica. Use this recipe (or substitute your own) to make a delicious, fruity drink:

3 c. (710 mL) orange juice
1 c. (240 mL) grapefruit juice
2 c. (470 mL) crushed ice
1 can crushed pineapple with juice

Put the juices and the ice in a blender and blend at the "ice crush" speed until well mixed. Stir in the can of crushed pineapple. Makes twelve 1/2 cup (120 mL) servings.

Chickens and Goats

Many farms in the Jamaican countryside raise chickens and goats. While the chickens are kept in coops, the goats are allowed to graze anywhere along the side of the road. At the end of the day, a farm child will go looking for and gather up all of the family's goats.

Make several copies of the Goat Herd pattern **(page 80)** on colored paper. Make two sets of each color. Cut out and laminate the cards. Make a necklace from one card of each color by punching a small hole at the top of the card and stringing a length of yarn through the hole. Scatter the goat cards around the room. Give each player a necklace along with instructions to find all of the goat cards that match. You may want to write numbers or vocabulary words on the backs of the goat cards. Then the children can put the cards in order (if numbered) or check the cards against a vocabulary list to make sure they have gathered all of the family's goats.

National Heroes Day

National Heroes Day is celebrated on the third Monday in October. This day is meant to honor seven people whose bravery and commitment to bettering life in Jamaica have made a difference in the lives of all Jamaicans. The seven honored heroes include Nanny, Sam Sharpe, George William Gordon, Paul Bogle, Marcus Garvey, Alexander Bustamante, and Norman Manely. Learn more about each of these people through books about Jamaica, then share their tales with the children. Discuss what it means to be a hero, and have the children write short essays about who they would nominate to be a hero for National Heroes Day.

Anansi the Spider

Children in Traditional Jamaican Dress

Flag of Jamaica

Directions: Color the diagonal cross gold. The top and bottom triangle are green. The other triangles are black.

Jamaican Postcard, Globe Marker,
Luggage Sticker, and Passport Stamp

Welcome to Jamaica, mon!

Postcard

Globe Marker

Luggage Sticker

Passport Stamp

Japan

Capital: Tokyo

Official Language: Japanese

Japan is located in the Pacific Ocean, just east of the Asian continent. The country is made up of several islands. Most people live on one of four main islands: Honshu, Kyushu, Hokkaido, or Shikoku. Japan is also very mountainous, which means there is not much farmland.

Because people in Japan bow their heads to greet one another, they have a reputation for being a very polite and honest people. The name Japan, or *Nippon* in Japanese, means "source of the sun." The country is often called "Land of the Rising Sun." Here are a few Japanese words and phrases to help you get started on your journey:

English	Japanese
Hello / Good afternoon	*Konnichiwa*
Good-bye	*Sayonara*
Please	*Onegai shimasu*
Thank you	*Arigato*
Yes	*Hai*
No	*Iie*
1 – one	*ichi*
2 – two	*ni*
3 – three	*san*
4 – four	*shi*
5 – five	*go*
6 – six	*roku*
7 – seven	*shichi*
8 – eight	*hachi*
9 – nine	*ku*
10 – ten	*ju*

For more information about Japan:

Embassy of Japan
2520 Massachusetts Avenue NW
Washington, DC 20008

Phone: (202) 238-6700
Fax: (202) 328-2187
http://www.us.emb-japan.go.jp/english/html/index.htm

Japanese Cuisine

If you have ever removed your shoes before entering someone's home or eaten at a knee-high table while you sit on the floor, you know what mealtime is like in Japan. A traditional Japanese table is set with drinking cups with no handles. Chopsticks are used for utensils, and the table might be set with a variety of cooked rice, fish, and perhaps a little bit of sushi (raw fish).

Prop some folding tables about 6" (15 cm) off the floor with books. Have the children remove their shoes, bow to one another upon greeting, and eat a snack of rice with chopsticks at your Japanese dinner table.

Shichi-Go-San

Odd numbers are considered lucky in Japan. If you look closely, you will notice that the name of this celebration is the same as the words for the numbers 7 (shichi), 5 (go), and 3 (san). November 15 is a special day for Japanese children. On this day, girls who are three and seven, and boys who are three and five dress up in their finest clothing and go to shrines to be blessed. In addition to a blessing of health and good fortune, the children also receive chitose-ame, or pieces of red and white candy, in white paper bags. The bags are usually decorated with symbols of good luck, such as the crane, tortoise, cricket, or bamboo.

Celebrate Shichi-go-san by decorating white paper bags with symbols of good luck. Press a pine bough into paint and gently press it onto the bags to make prints. Draw pictures of other good-luck symbols like bamboo, cranes, or tortoises. Make chitose-ame out of red and white chenille stems. Twist the stems together to make long sticks of candy. Let the children create their own bags and chitose-ame as souvenirs of their visit to Japan.

Cricket

The cricket is another good-luck symbol in Japan. Many people keep crickets in small cages in their homes. The cheerful chirp of the cricket is said to ward off evil and bring good luck. Make a copy of the Lucky Cricket pattern **(page 107)** on heavy card stock for each child. Have the children color and cut out the cages, cutting out the spaces between the bars as well. Laminate the cages and cut along the dotted lines at the top with a craft knife. Staple or glue each cage to a second sheet of card stock and trim it down to the same shape. Have the children color their crickets and place them in the cages. Hang the cages from the ceiling throughout your celebration.

Turn the cricket page into a file folder game by mounting the laminated cricket cage onto a file folder. Remove the flap closure of a large envelope, and glue the envelope below the cage as shown. Laminate the entire file folder and the cage. Being careful not to cut the folder beneath, cut a slit at the top of the cage where indicated by the dotted line, and across the top of the envelope so that items can be slipped in and out of the pocket. Write a word ending at the top of a 4" x 6" (10 cm x 15 cm) index card. Make several copies of the crickets and write rhyming words on them. For example, write "ed" on a card, and "bed," "red," etc. on the crickets. You can use more challenging rhymes with older children, including words that rhyme but are spelled differently, such as "head" or "said."

Laminate the cards and the crickets. Make additional sets of rhyming cards and crickets and place them in separate zippered plastic bags.

To play, spread all of the crickets faceup on the table, and place a word ending card in the pocket. The child looks for all of the crickets that rhyme with the sound and puts them in the cage. Repeat with other rhymes.

Origami

Origami is the Japanese art of paper folding. Make a copy of the Origami Pagoda pattern **(page 108)** for each child, or cut 6" (15 cm) squares out of colorful or patterned paper. Have the children cut out the squares and color both sides of the paper any way they wish. Fold the paper pagodas as directed on page 108. A pagoda is the name of a Japanese temple or shrine—it is another symbol of good luck. Glue the origami pagodas on sheets of construction paper. Add other figures, such as the rising sun, mountains, and Japanese people, to complete the scenes. Select a book on origami from your local library and try other folding projects.

Boy's Day

May 5 is traditionally known as Boy's Day in Japan. This is a day in which families celebrate the boys in the family. Each family flies a series of kites at their home, each kite in the shape of a koi, or carp (a type of fish). The top fish is the largest and represents the eldest son, and each additional fish is gradually smaller representing each of the other boys in the home. Make copies of the Koi Kite pattern **(page 109)** in graduated sizes by copying at 90%, 80%, 70%, and 60%.

Have the children create a sequenced koi kite by coloring one of each size of fish. Have them tape the fish in descending order of size on a piece of string and then tie the string to a stick. Extend the activity to have the children make koi pole kites to represent their own families, using large fish for the adults and increasingly smaller fish for siblings.

Doll's Day

Doll's Day, or Girl's Day, is celebrated on March 3. On this day, girls bring their special dolls to a tea. These dolls are often handcrafted and have been passed down from one generation to the next. Since they are so delicate and special, the dolls are rarely used and are quickly wrapped up and tucked away for the next year's celebration. To celebrate Doll's Day, have each child bring in a favorite doll, stuffed animal, or special gift given by a relative. Ask the children to share why those dolls or animals are special to them, and then have everyone sit on the floor for a Doll's Day tea party. Serve juice and rice cakes, and encourage the children to offer some to their dolls, too.

Torii

A torii is a special gate that guards the entrance to a temple, shrine, or even harbor. It is considered good luck to sail or cross under a torii. A torii consists of two side bars that support two crossbars. Cut four large strips of paper: one that measures 1/2' x 4' (0.15 m x 1.22 m), a second that is 1/2' x 6' (0.15 m x 1.83 m), and two more that are 1/2' x 8' (0.15 m x 2.44 m). Use these pieces to make a torii at the entrance to your classroom. Place the 8' (2.44 m) strips along the sides of the door. Lay the 4' (1.22 m) strip across the top of the door and across the side strips. Place the 6' (1.83 m) strip above the 4' (1.22 m) strip and across the two side strips. Have the children help you decorate the torii with pine boughs and other good-luck symbols.

Karesansui

A *karesansui* is a Japanese rock garden. Gravel, stones, and sometimes moss are arranged to represent landforms such as islands, rivers, and mountains. All of the rocks are raked into patterns. This type of gardening is popular among those who practice the religion of Zen Buddhism. They believe that people can learn things when they work hard and meditate. These two attributes are the focus when creating a karesansui garden.

Collect one shoe-box lid for each child. Have the children fill the bottoms of the boxes with small rocks. Encourage the children to rake through the rocks with forks to create patterns of waves, swirls, and circles. Add a few larger rocks or bits of grass and moss for interest. Place the completed gardens on a table for viewing, and encourage the children to rearrange their gardens as they wish.

Sumo Wrestling

Sumo wrestling is one of the national sports of Japan. Sumo wrestlers are very large and consider it a great honor to wrestle for Japan. Wrestlers who do not do well are expected to retire so they do not bring shame to the sport. A wrestling match occurs between two wrestlers in a 15' circular ring. The first player to put any part of his body (besides the soles of his feet) down on the mat is out.

Punch two holes in the bottom of a large garbage bag. Have a child slip his legs through the holes and pull the bag up to his shoulders. Stuff the bag full of crumpled newspaper and tie it closed just under the child's arms to simulate the bulk of a sumo wrestler. Make a second sumo wrestler costume. Then have the children take turns trying to wrestle one another out of a circular ring created with tape on the floor. Give everyone who shows valiant effort a gold medal.

Geisha

Geisha girls are the well-recognized women with white faces, tight hair buns, and kimonos who are trained in singing and dancing. Geisha dancers often perform for royalty and special ceremonies. Hand fans or other props are sometimes incorporated into the smooth, slow movements of the dance. Have everyone make a hand fan by coloring a sheet of construction paper as desired. Place the paper facedown on the table, fold over the top 1" (25 mm) , and crease the fold. Continue to fold the paper back and forth, accordion-style, until the fan is folded completely. Find a selection of Japanese music and have the children create and perform their own geisha dances.

Shogatsu

Shogatsu (also called *oshogatsu*) is the Japanese New Year. Japan celebrates the New Year with customs similar to those in other countries around the world. Houses are cleaned and decorated with pine, bamboo and plum branches. Bonenkai ("Forget the year") parties are held to say good-bye to the old year. People get up early to watch the sun rise on the first day of the New Year, and everyone makes an effort to keep the day happy. This ensures that the year to come will be equally pleasant. Many people visit shrines, fly kites, play games, and send New Year's cards to celebrate the New Year.

Have the children create New Year's cards on 4" x 6" (10 cm x 15 cm) index cards for each classmate. Sort out the cards and deliver the stacks to the children on the day you celebrate the New Year holiday.

Read *The Emperor and the Kite* by Jane Yolen (Philomel, 1988) or other stories about flying kites. If the weather permits, go outside and try flying a kite. Otherwise, have the children design their own kites indoors with tissue paper and streamers.

Fuku Warai

Fuku warai is a fun game often played by children during the Shogatsu celebrations. To play you will need to cut out several facial features from old magazines. Place the different eyes, eyebrows, ears, noses, and mouths in separate bags. Draw a Fuku warai face pattern by making an outline of a head with no features on a sheet of paper. Make a copy of the pattern for each child. Have the children work in teams of two or three, each choosing a set of eyes, eyebrows, ears, mouth, and nose from the prepared bags. Blindfold the first player. Have another player put a dot of glue on the back of the first facial feature (e.g., an eye) and then hand the piece to the blindfolded player. That child then tries to stick the eye in the correct place on the head pattern. Other players may give verbal clues (e.g., "to the left" or "down"), but the blindfolded player may not touch the paper with her hands. Repeat with the other facial pieces and then switch roles so the other children each have turns. Have a good laugh when sharing the skewed Fuku warai faces with everyone.

Ukiyo-e

Many pieces of beautiful Japanese artwork are created through a process called ukiyo-e. ukiyo-e is the handicraft of the woodblock print. It takes three people to create a work of art in this manner: an artist, a carver, and a printer. This form of woodblock painting provides a way to mass-produce art: once the block has been created, it can be used over and over again without having to redraw the image.

Divide the class into teams of three to work on a simplified version of the Ukiyo-e process. Assign one person to be the artist, the second the carver, and the third the printer. Give the artist a 2" x 3" (5 cm x 8 cm) sheet of tissue paper. Have him draw a simple pattern on the tissue. Next have the carver place the pattern over a bar of Ivory® soap. (Ivory is used because it is soft enough to carve easily.). Using a sharp pencil, the carver traces over the design to transfer it onto the soap, and then carves the soap with a sturdy plastic knife. Once the design has been created, the printer uses paint or an ink pad to stamp the design onto several pages. Have everyone switch roles and let a new artist begin the process again. Print this new piece of art onto the same pages already printed. Share one piece of the completed art with the team members and use the others for making New Year's cards **(see page 105, Shogatsu).**

Lucky Cricket

Origami Pagoda

1. Fold the paper in half to make a crease.
2. Open the fold and fold the paper in half horizontally.
3. Fold the edges (A) to the center crease (B).
4. Open up the fold (C) and press.
5. Repeat with the other side.

Step 1

Step 2

Step 3

Step 4

Step 5

Koi Kite

Children in Traditional Japanese Dress

Flag of Japan

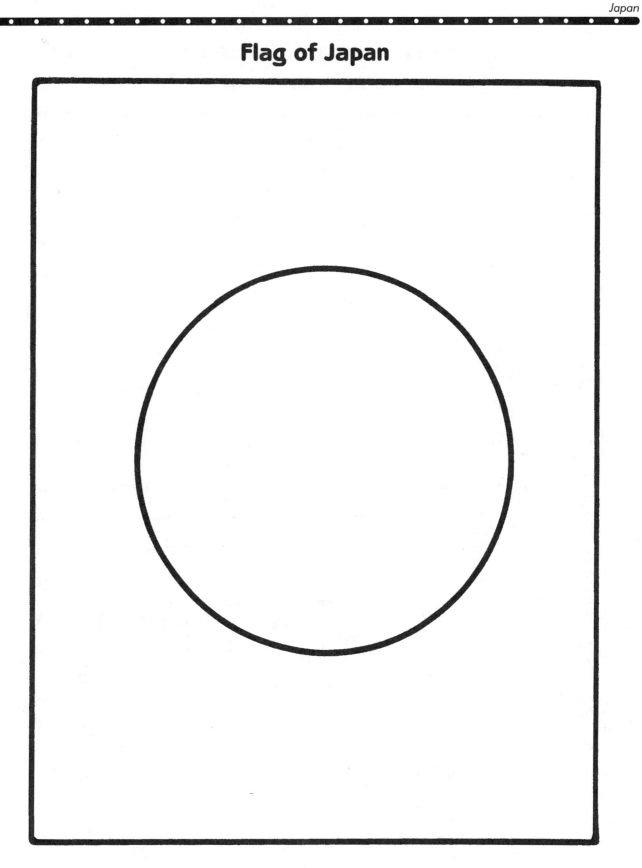

Directions: The background of the flag is white. Color the circle red.

Japanese Postcard, Globe Marker,
Luggage Sticker, and Passport Stamp

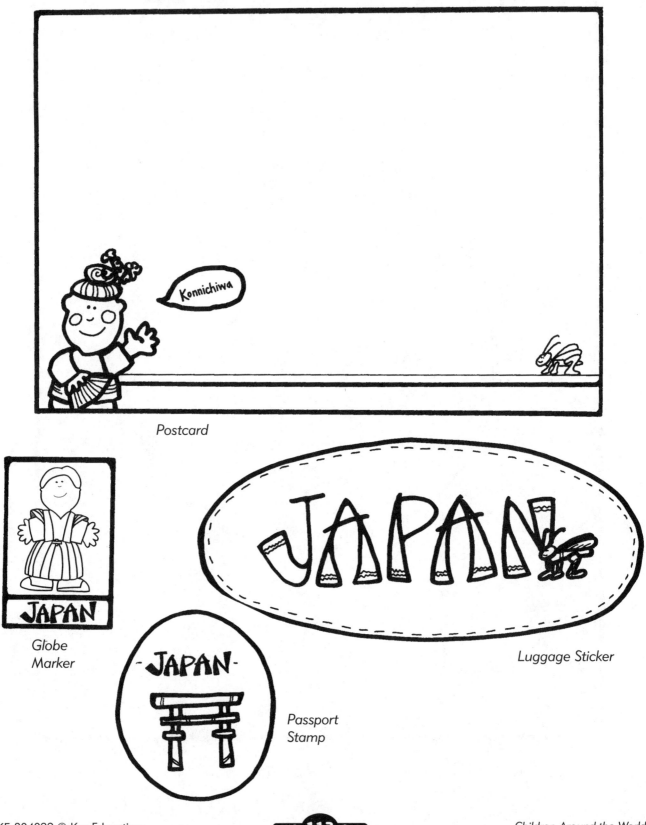

Postcard

Globe
Marker

Passport
Stamp

Luggage Sticker

Mexico

Capital: Mexico City
Official Language: Spanish

¡Buenos días! Greetings from Mexico! Mexico is located in North America. While children of Mexico enjoy playing just like children of all countries, there are many customs and celebrations that are unique to Mexico.

Enjoy your visit to Mexico! Here are a few Spanish phrases and numbers to help you get started:

English	Spanish
Hello	*Hola*
Good-bye	*Adiós*
Please	*Por favor*
Thank you	*Gracias*
Yes	*Sí*
No	*No*
1 – one	*uno*
2 – two	*dos*
3 – three	*tres*
4 – four	*cuatro*
5 – five	*cinco*
6 – six	*seis*
7 – seven	*siete*
8 – eight	*ocho*
9 – nine	*nueve*
10 – ten	*diez*

For more information about Mexico:

Embassy of Mexico
1911 Pennsylvania Avenue NW
Washington, DC 20006

Phone: (202) 728-1600
Fax: (202) 728-1698
http://portal.sre.gob.mx/usa/

Fiesta!

¡Viva México! Long Live Mexico! It's time to celebrate! There are many special holidays and remembrances that are celebrated by children in Mexico. Check out *Fiesta!* by Ginger Foglesong Guy (Greenwillow Books, 1996) or other books on Mexico, and let the children explore the pictures and language of the people of Mexico. Then combine any of the fun activities included in this chapter to create your own classroom fiesta. You may want to learn about Mexico on one of the holidays listed below:

- January 17, Day of Saint Anthony the Abbot — In honor of this saint, the children dress their animals (dogs, chickens, cats, goats, birds, etc.) in festive costumes and parade them to the churches. There the priests give the animals special blessings. Have your own parade of (stuffed) animals or pets to start off your celebration.

- May 5, Cinco de Mayo — This is the day Mexico celebrates its victory over the French army (1862).

- September 16, Mexican Independence Day — Mexico celebrates its independence from Spain (1821) on this day.

Piñatas

Children break open piñatas at celebrations for special holidays and birthdays. While piñatas can be quite ornate and come in a variety of shapes, you may wish to choose a more simple approach. To make a basic piñata, decorate a large brown paper bag with colorful crepe paper. Glue a few streamers around the bottom edge of the bag. Insert a second or third bag inside the decorated bag for added strength. Fill the innermost bag with small toys and candy. Lay a 4' (1.22 m) length of rope along the top edge of the bag and fold the bag over it two or three times. Secure the folded edge with staples or packing tape. Knot the ends of the rope together and hang the piñata from a tree (or tie it to the end of a broom handle). Have the children take turns swinging a plastic bat at the piñata while blindfolded. Once the piñata is split open, the children can share the goodies that were hidden inside.

You can also have the children create their own piñatas to decorate the classroom. Repeat the steps listed above using brown paper lunch bags. Decorate as desired and stuff with newspaper. Fold over the tops of the bags and staple shut. Hang your piñatas from the ceiling as decorations.

Confetti Eggs

Save halved eggshells from another cooking project, or have the children's parents save them for you. Carefully and gently dye the empty eggshells by dipping them in a solution of 1 cup (240 mL) warm water, 2 tablespoons (10 mL) vinegar, and food coloring. (See the back of the food coloring package for suggestions on creating different colors.) While the eggshells are drying, give each child a pair of scissors and some scrap paper. Have the children cut the scrap paper into small confetti pieces. Fill the shells half full with confetti, then cover the open end of each egg with a 2" square (5 cm) piece of crepe paper. Glue the paper in place to hold the confetti inside the egg.

During your celebration, the children can crack the confetti eggs over the heads of their classmates for good luck.

Serapes

A serape is a large woven shawl that is worn over the head and shoulders. While it takes many hours to weave an authentic serape out of brightly dyed wool, you can create a simple serape out of craft paper or a large brown paper bag.

You will need one large sheet of craft paper about 4' or 5' long (1.22 m or 1.52 m) for each serape. Fold the sheet in half and find the center of the fold. Cut a 9" (23 cm) "V" near the center of the fold. Have the children decorate their serapes by coloring or painting bold stripes and patterns the entire length and width of the paper. Cut 3" (8 cm) slits along the bottom edge of the serape to create a fringe border.

Sombreros

The sombrero is a very common hat in Mexico. Its wide brim helps keep the hot sun off the head and shoulders. Make your own decorated sombrero for your fiesta. Have the children work in teams to create sombreros for each other. Lay a large sheet of craft paper over the head of one child. Have two or more children hold the paper on the head while another wraps a long string of masking tape over the paper around the crown of the head. Begin rolling the paper upward around the hat. You may have to tape, glue, or trim a couple of edges. Paint the sombreros bright colors and decorate them with sequins, jewels, and ribbons. Play a copy of the song "Mexican Hat Dance." Invite the children to dance to the music while wearing their sombreros and serapes. Toss your sombreros in the air and dance around them as they land on the floor.

Mariachi Band

Mariachi bands are popular entertainers at celebrations in Mexico. A mariachi band is a small group of strolling musicians. A band typically includes a violin, a trumpet, and some guitars.

Divide the class into several mariachi bands. Have the students make their own musical instruments in class or use real classroom instruments to make music. Take turns strolling and entertaining during your celebration. You can also take your bands on a tour throughout the school to entertain other classes.

Tortillas

    4 c. (950 mL) flour
    1 tbsp. (15 mL) baking powder
    1 tsp. (5 mL) salt
    1/4 c. (60 mL) shortening
    1 c. (240 mL) lukewarm water

Mix flour, baking powder, and salt together in a large mixing bowl. Cut in the shortening. Add 1 cup of the water to the mix and stir to make the dough. Add more water as needed (the dough should feel soft and pliable—about like your earlobe). Divide the dough into 3" (8 cm) balls and roll out each ball into a thin circle. Cook in a skillet over medium heat, turning often until both sides are lightly browned.

Spread butter on the warm tortillas and sprinkle with cinnamon and sugar, or dip the tortillas in salsa. Store any unused tortillas in an airtight container.

Tortilla Toss

Use masking tape to create several 2' (61 cm) square goal boxes on the floor of the play area along the perimeter. Write a different numeral (e.g., "2") or math sentence (e.g., "2 + 3 =") on a large index card to put in each goal. Cut several large circles from heavy card stock or use paper plates as tortillas. To play this game, a child stands with a partner in the middle of the play area. Players take turns tossing the same number of tortillas into each goal as indicated by the numeral on the card or the answer to the math sentence. Each tortilla that lands inside the outlines of the goal is worth one point. Have the children help each other check their tossing and counting.

Silver Jewelry

Silver is a metal that is abundant in Mexico. As a result, jewelry made from silver is very common. To make your own silver medallions, cut shapes out of Styrofoam plates. Cover the shapes with small scraps of aluminum foil and secure the edges on the back with pieces of transparent tape. Turn the medallions over and have the children "scratch" designs on the fronts with dull pencils. Poke a hole in the top of each medallion and string a paper clip through the hole. Hang the finished medallions on pieces of string or yarn and tie them around the children's necks.

To create beads, cut several small strips of aluminum foil. Carefully wrap and then mold the foil strips into tiny ball shapes around the string. Add additional foil balls, colored beads, and other medallions as desired.

Story Murals

Diego Rivera was one of Mexico's most famous artists. He painted many beautiful murals that depicted the history of Mexico and the Mexican people. Have the children create their own murals, first by writing or dictating stories about themselves. Have the children read through their stories again, highlighting or circling important people, places, or things. Have them illustrate their stories on large sheets of craft paper. Encourage each child to fill the entire page with images from the story and to color the images with pastels, chalk, crayons, or paint.

Have the children share their mural stories with the other children in class. See if the others can help tell each story by studying the pictures in the mural. Then have the children read their stories to the class. Hang the finished murals and stories around the classroom for everyone to enjoy.

Ancient Pottery

Inspired by Aztec designs, Mexican pottery is often painted with intricate patterns or with images of local culture. Bring an illustrated book about Mexican pottery to class, and let the children study the different patterns and pictures on the pottery pieces.

Many of the clay pots once used by the Aztec people have been unearthed by archaeologists. Often the specimens are broken and must be pieced back together to recreate the original vessels. Paint several clay pots with pastels, crayons, paints, or gel markers. Spray with a fixative to preserve the artwork. Then carefully break the pots into several large pieces. Bury the pots in a small sand pile or large container of sand. Provide several small spoons and paintbrushes for the children to use in excavating the pot pieces. See if they can reassemble the pots by matching the colors and patterns on the pieces.

Siesta Time

For many Mexicans, the biggest meal of the day is served around midday. Afterward, it is not uncommon for people to take a rest for a couple of hours during the heat of the day. They then return to work late in the afternoon and work until evening. This period of rest is called a siesta (see-ES-tah). To play the siesta game, give each child a small paper bowl. Place a few dried beans in each bowl, and then have the children lie on their backs with their eyes closed. Place the bowls on the floor next to their heads. Choose one or two children to be "It." Those who are "It" must try to steal the beans from the other players' bowls without getting caught. If a child who is taking a siesta hears the beans being removed from her bowl, she can say "¡STOP, por favor!" The beans must then be returned to the child. After a predetermined time, call an end to the game and count the beans taken during the siesta. Graph the results and play again.

Poetic Pyramids

The ancient Aztecs built great pyramids out of stone. The silhouettes of these pyramids created a stair-step pattern that is often repeated in the artwork and architecture of modern-day Mexico.

Create poetic pyramids by cutting 1" (25 mm) strips of colored paper into five different lengths. Beginning at the bottom of a sheet of construction paper, glue the strips in order from longest to shortest, centering each strip as you go. Have the children draw pictures of themselves at the tops of the pyramids, then follow these steps to write their pyramid poems: Leave the top step of the pyramid blank. Write your name on the second strip. On the strip below that, write the names of two of your favorite things. On the fourth strip, write three words ending in "ing" that describe your favorite things. On the bottom strip, complete the phrase "Always _____, never _____." to describe yourself. Add the finished poems to the Travel Journals.

Sean

trucks, motorbikes

jumping, running, playing

Always happy, never sad

Bullfight

Bullfighting is a very popular sport in Mexico. It can also be a very dangerous sport. Try a fun (and safe!) adaptation of this pastime in your own classroom. Begin by making a copy of the Bullfighter Game pattern **(page 118)** on heavy card stock. Color the game board as desired. Color each bull a different color. Cut out the game board and bull playing pieces, and assemble the game board. Then laminate all of the game pieces.

Glue the game board to the inside of a file folder, leaving the top square free of glue. Fold the conquistador up along the dotted line so that he stands when the file folder is on a flat surface. Fold the flaps at the bottom of each bull piece along the dotted lines to allow the pieces to stand on their own. Tape the flaps together in back if necessary

To play, place the bulls on the square labeled "Start." The youngest player begins and rolls a die. If she rolls an even number, she moves her bull that many spaces forward. If she rolls an odd number, she moves that many spaces backward. Players take turns rolling the die and moving their game pieces. The first player whose bull reaches the conquistador wins the game. He gets to stand up and take a bow before his adoring fans.

Bullfighter Game

To assemble the game board, tape or glue the two strips together, overlapping the striped area.

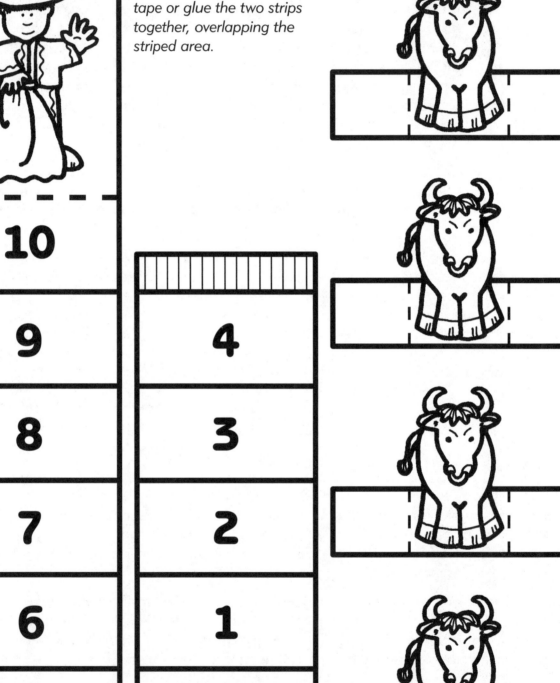

10
9
8
7
6
5

4
3
2
1
Start

Children in Traditional Mexican Dress

Flag of Mexico

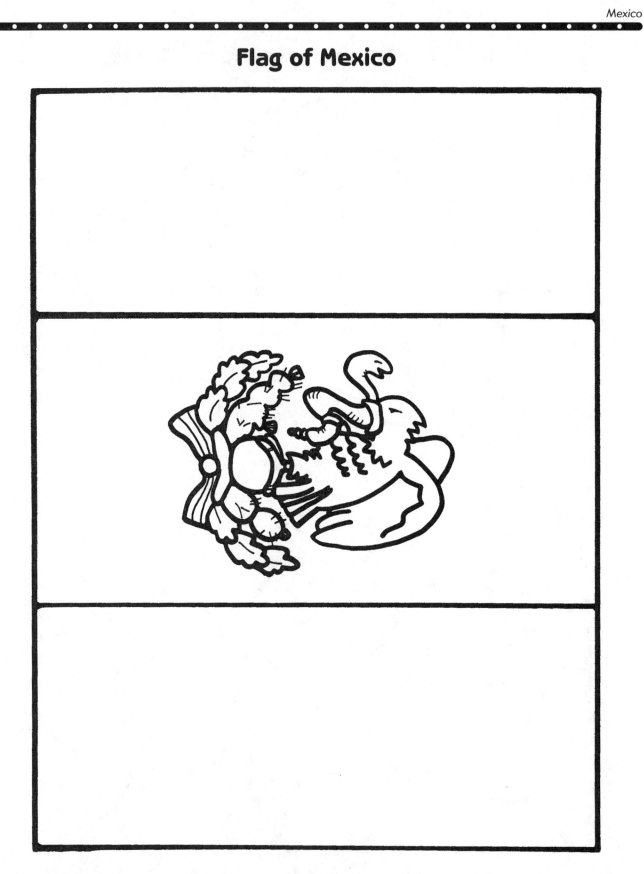

Directions: Color the stripes of the flag: green, white, and red (left to right). Make the eagle brown. Color the snake and cactus green.

Mexican Postcard, Globe Marker,
Luggage Sticker, and Passport Stamp

Postcard

Globe
Marker

Luggage
Sticker

Passport
Stamp

Russia

Capital: Moscow

Official Language: Russian

Russia, also known as the Russian Federation, is the largest country on Earth in total land area. It covers the globe all the way from Europe in the east, across the entire northern part of Asia, until it finally reaches the Pacific Ocean in the west.

Here are a few Russian words and phrases to help you get started on your journey:

English	Russian
Hi / Hello	Privet
Good-bye	Do svidaniya
Thank you	Spasibo
Please	Pazhaluysta
Yes	Da
No	Net
1 – one	odin
2 – two	dva
3 – three	tri
4 – four	chetyre
5 – five	pyat
6 – six	shest
7 – seven	sem
8 – eight	vosem
9 – nine	devyat
10 – ten	desyat

For more information about Russia:

Embassy of the Russian Federation
2650 Wisconsin Avenue NW
Washington, DC 20007

Phone: (202) 298-5700
Fax: (202) 298-5735
http://www.russianembassy.org/

Slova

The Russian word *slova* means "words" in English. Russian children often play word games such as seeing how many words they can make out of longer words. Write "Welcome to Russia!" on the chalkboard. Give the children five minutes to see how many words they can build using only the letters in that phrase. Then write a second word on the board: "zdravstvuyte," which is another way to say "hello." See how many words the children can make out of these letters.

Siberia

Siberia is on the northern edge of Russia. It is very cold there, and people may not see the sun for months during wintertime. Many years ago, a person who fell into disfavor with the government might have been banished to Siberia to live. The harsh conditions there were considered a great punishment.

Play a fun game called "Banished to Siberia" using a deck of cards and a pair of mittens. Two to four players can play at a time. Shuffle the cards and deal the entire deck facedown to all players. Player #1 turns over the card from the bottom of her stack and places it faceup on the table. Play continues with each player drawing a card from the bottom of his stack and placing it in the middle of the table. If a player draws an ace, she is "banished to Siberia" and must put the mittens on in order to keep warm. Maneuvering with the mittens will be considerably more difficult, much as life is for those who brave the winters in Siberia. Play continues as before until a second ace is drawn. If a different player drew the ace, that player now puts on the mittens. The game continues until all four aces have been played. The player who is wearing the mittens at the end of the game has to clean up after everyone else. To extend the game, choose a new card or multiple cards to be the "banished to Siberia" card(s), or add other winter clothing to be worn each time a chosen card is played.

A Kopeck for Your Thoughts?

When a person wants to know what someone else is thinking, they might ask, "A penny for your thoughts?" But in Russia, they do not use pennies. Instead, they have kopecks. One hundred kopecks are equal to one ruble, which is the Russian unit of currency. So, perhaps while visiting Russia, you might get asked, "A kopeck for your thoughts?" Write the phrase "A kopeck for your thoughts?" across the top of a sheet of paper and make one copy for each child in class. Explain what the question is asking (i.e., "What are you thinking about?") and tell the class that you will be asking them that question throughout the day. Each time you ask the question, have the children stop what they are doing and write down what they are thinking about at that very moment. You may wish to encourage the children to share some of the more poignant or humorous thoughts with the entire class at the end of the day.

Grandma Babushka

In Russia, children often live with their parents and their grandparents. The Russian word for grandmother is *babushka*. Read *Babushka Baba Yaga* by Patricia Polacco (Philomel, 1993). Then let the children share tales of their own grandmothers or share their favorite things to do with their grandparents. Encourage each child to bring in a favorite toy, book, picture, or special treasure

from his or her babushka. Make a copy of the Grandma Babushka pattern **(page 127)** for each child. Have the children draw pictures of their grandmothers and include short notes that follow the prompt, "Grandma Babushka, I love you because . . ."

Since many elderly Russian women wear scarves to cover their heads, these scarves have also come to be known as babushkas. Cut an 18" (46 cm) square of white fabric, or purchase a white scarf or handkerchief for each child. Have the children use fabric paints to stamp and decorate their babushkas. The finished projects can be given as gifts to grandmothers if desired.

Chess

Chess is a popular game in Russia. Public parks are often filled with tables of chess players competing to see who can be the next champion. Gather a couple of chess sets and teach the children how to play the game. It may take a few reminders, but the children can learn the complex moves of the game. A simple game of checkers may be the best bet for younger players.

Children's Day

Children's Day in Russia is all about saying good-bye to winter and hello to spring. Ice-skating, sleigh riding, eating good food, parading around town, and other forms of revelry mark the day. Occasionally, a winter scarecrow will be built and then burned to symbolize the end of winter. Enjoy these fun activities to say good-bye to winter and welcome spring:

- Take off your shoes and "skate" around the floor (a hard surface works best) in your socks for some ice-skating fun.

- If there is snow where you live, build a snowman and then have fun smashing it apart.

- If you do not have snow on the ground, make a snowman out of white craft paper. Cover the nearby walls and floor with a tarp or plastic covering. Load some small sponges with pastel paints, and let the children toss the sponges at the snowman until it is completely covered in spring colors.

- Tie a rope around a laundry basket or old box, and tie sleigh bells to the sides of the box. Have the children pull one another around the room for sleigh rides. Build two sleighs and let the children race one another.

- Dress up in your winter outerwear, play musical instruments, and parade around the school, shedding your heavy winter gear as you go.

Brrr . . . Verkhoyansk

Verkhoyansk is one of the coldest places on Earth. Verkhoyansk is found in Siberia near the Arctic Circle. Temperatures there dip well below zero for many days of the year and can even reach as low as -90°F (-68°C). As a class, make a list of as many things as possible that are cold. Make a second list of as many ways as possible to get warm.

What is the temperature where you are? Gather several small, non-mercury thermometers and let the children decide where to place them. (Encourage them to think of places where the temperatures may differ, such as outside in the shade, in the sun, or in a refrigerator.) Is the hall

colder than your classroom? Is your room colder than the room next door? Put a thermometer in each place and let the thermometers acclimate for one hour. Return later and check the temperature on each thermometer. Discuss your findings as a class.

For one week, keep a graph of the outdoor temperature at your school. Who knows, your city may be the next coldest city on Earth!

Happy New Year

Happy New Year! Or, as spoken in Russian, "S novim godom!" One of the most important holidays celebrated in Russia is the New Year. In 1917, the czar of Russia banned Christmas. People began celebrating the New Year instead, but many of the traditions are remarkably similar to the traditions of Christmas. See if your class recognizes a few familiar people and symbols in the Russian New Year's celebration:

- Families come from great distances to gather together to celebrate the New Year.

- A pine tree is brought into the home and decorated.

- At the stroke of midnight, chimes ring out, heralding in the New Year.

- Music, dancing, good food, and revelry last on into the New Year.

- Grandfather Frost visits the children overnight and leaves gifts.

- Grandfather Frost's daughter, Snowmaiden, helps him prepare the gifts.

Although Russia celebrates the New Year on December 31 and January 1, you can have your own Russian New Year's Celebration any time of the year.

- Have each child bring in a gently used book or toy for a class gift exchange.

- Borrow an artificial Christmas tree (or cut a large tree shape out of green craft paper) and set it up in the classroom as a "New Year's tree." Let the children make ornaments to decorate it.

- Have the children make lists of New Year's wishes for Grandfather Frost.

Rye Bread

One of the most popular types of bread in Russia is rye bread. Collect an assortment of different kinds of breads, including rye, and break each one into bite-sized pieces. Ask the children to sample the pieces and see if they can identify the rye bread. Take a vote to see which bread was the most popular among the children.

Painted Eggs

During the Easter season, Russians enjoy decorating hard-boiled eggs. First they give the eggs an overall color, like ochre (yellowish-brown). Then they paint or draw delicate, intricate patterns on the eggs. To make your own painted eggs, hard-boil enough fresh eggs to have at least one for each child. (You may want to have some extras on hand for the occasional mishap.) Dip a cotton ball into yellow paint and paint a small section of an egg by rubbing in a small, circular motion. Dip

a cotton-tipped swab into brown paint and dot it on top of the yellow paint. Rub the brown paint into the yellow paint in small, circular motions. Continue adding yellow and dabs of brown until the egg is a beautiful ochre color. Have the children color their eggs the same way. Allow the eggs to dry thoroughly. Then, using permanent markers or gel pens, draw small designs all over the eggs. Later, you can carefully peel away the eggshells, saving some of your artwork, and enjoy your hard-boiled egg for a snack.

Variation: A more lasting alternative to this project is to remove the insides of the eggs, leaving the outer shells intact for painting. To do this, carefully poke a hole with a large needle in each end of the uncooked eggs. Gently blow on one end of each egg until all of the egg matter comes out the other end. If blowing is particularly difficult or unproductive, you may need to enlarge the bottom hole slightly. Run warm water through the eggs until it comes out clean. Shake or blow any remaining water out of the eggs and let them dry overnight before painting.

Matryoshka Dolls

The Matryoshka doll is a popular toy from Russia. This doll is carved from wood and opens at the middle to reveal a second doll inside, slightly smaller than the first. This doll in turn has another doll inside of it, and so on until there is only one small doll, too small to divide.

Make your own paper Matryoshka dolls by copying the Matryoshka Dolls pattern **(page 128)** onto heavy card stock. Have the children color the dolls as desired, keeping in mind that each doll within a set should look just like the others. Carefully cut around the solid black border of each doll. Bead a very thin line of glue around the edge of the largest doll and glue it to a second sheet of heavy card stock paper. Repeat this process with each of the smaller dolls. Allow the glue to dry completely. Trim the back sheets of card stock on each doll to just a hair wider than the doll outline on the front. Then carefully cut the three largest dolls in half by cutting along the dotted lines. Do not cut the smallest doll in half.

Place the smallest doll inside the bottom half of the next larger doll. Fit the top over the small doll to meet the bottom half. Repeat with the other dolls until all of the dolls are tucked inside the largest one.

Gorodki

Gorodki is a fun Russian bowling game. Mark a 3' (0.9 m) circle on the floor with masking tape. Mark a second circle, this one about 4' (1.22 m) in diameter, about 20' (6 m) away from the first one. Stack five pegs inside the second circle. (Empty steel or aluminum cans work well for this. Just decorate them for added interest.) Roll up several sheets of newspaper and wrap them with heavy packing or duct tape to form a dowel-shaped rod, or bat. Make two bats.

Have the children take turns standing in the first circle and tossing bats at the second circle. The object of the game is to knock all of the pegs out of the circle. Just like in bowling, each player gets two attempts per turn. Score one point for each peg knocked completely out of the circle.

Grandma Babushka

Grandma Babushka, I love you because . . .

Matryoshka Dolls

128

Children in Traditional Russian Dress

Flag of Russia

Directions: Color the stripes of the flag: white, black, and red (top to bottom).

Russian Postcard, Globe Marker,
Luggage Sticker, and Passport Stamp

Postcard

Luggage Sticker

Passport Stamp

Globe Marker

Scotland

Capital: Edinburgh
Official Language: English (Scottish Gaelic also spoken)

Scotland is part of the United Kingdom, and so it is ruled by the Prime Minister and Queen of England. The Scottish countryside is made up of the Highlands (steep mountains and narrow valleys called *glens*), the Central Lowlands (low hills and fields), and the Southern Uplands (boggy areas with no trees called *moors*). Most of the countryside is covered in grass, which turns to a vibrant purple color in the spring when the heather blooms. As Scotland is flanked by the Atlantic Ocean, it has many *firths* (bays) and is also home to many *lochs* (lakes).

Now that you have learned a few Scottish geography terms, here are some other words and phrases to help you on your journey:

English	Scottish Gaelic
Hello	*Halò*
Good-bye	*Beannachd leibh*
Thank you	*Tapadh leibh*
1 – one	*aon*
2 – two	*dhà*
3 – three	*trì*
4 – four	*ceithir*
5 – five	*còig*
6 – six	*sia*
7 – seven	*seachd*
8 – eight	*ochd*
9 – nine	*naoi*
10 – ten	*deich*

Source: http://www.bbc.co.uk/scotland/alba/foghlam/beag_air_bheag/index.shtml

For more information about Scotland:

Public Affairs Team
The British Embassy – Washington D.C.
3100 Massachusetts Avenue NW
Washington, DC 20008-3600

Phone: (900) 255-6685
http://www.britainusa.com/

Celtic Warriors

The Celts (pronounced KELTS) were fierce warriors who occupied Scotland many years ago. When the Romans tried to invade Scotland, the Celts fought them off. In order to keep the Celts from invading their newly acquired lands in Europe, the Romans built a huge wall across the island of Great Britain from coast to coast. This wall, called Hadrian's Wall (after Emperor Hadrian) stretches nearly 73 miles (117 kilometers) long, and most of it still stands today.

Build your own Hadrian's wall with wood blocks. Have the children take turns rolling a pair of dice. Whatever number appears on the dice, add that same number of blocks to your wall. Continue rolling and constructing until you have created a wall that extends the entire length of the classroom. Add additional layers to the wall as time and supplies allows.

Scottish Clans

The Scots are very proud of their heritage. Each family is part of a larger group of related families called clans. Each clan has its own tartan. A tartan is a pattern woven in cloth. People often wear clothing made from the plaid patterns of their clans' tartans.

Divide the class into small groups or clans. Instruct each clan to create their own tartan pattern using paper and markers rather than wool thread. Cut the tartan designs into squares and make name tags for all of the clan members. Have the children divide into their clans for group activities throughout your visit to Scotland.

Kilts

Most boys do not wear skirts, but men in Scotland are proud to wear them. Their skirts are actually called kilts, and they are typically made out of the tartan cloths of their clans. Kilts are typically worn for special occasions or festivals.

Collect a brown paper bag for each child. Cut the bags open down one side and then cut off the bottoms of the bags. Have the children make their own tartan patterns by drawing horizontal and vertical stripes with different colors of paint. Allow the paint to dry. Wrap the painted bags around the children's waists. Make pleats as needed for fit, and staple the kilts in position. Put a piece of reinforcing tape at the top corners of each tartan where they meet around the waist of the child. Punch a hole through the tape and tie the two ends together with a piece of yarn or rope. Have the class wear their kilts in a special celebration or while listening to some music performed by bagpipes.

Castles

Many years ago, people who lived in Scotland built and lived in huge castles. There are over 600 castles in Scotland today. As the country grew more populated, modern buildings sprang up all around these castles, so you can travel through a city and often find a castle right in the middle of town!

Play a game in which the children build their own castles. Copy the Castles Game Board patterns **(page 137 and 138)**. Arrange the pages on a sheet of poster board.

Make 12 copies of the Castle Game Piece pattern, shown next to this activity for each player. Each group of 12 castles should be printed on a different color paper. Cut out all of the castles. Laminate the game board and the castle pieces. Use small math manipulatives for game tokens. To play, give each clan a game token and all of the castles of one color. Clans take turns rolling a die, then moving their tokens the number of spaces indicated on the face of the die. If a player lands on a space with no written directions or another player's castle on it, the clan can tape one of their colored castles in that spot. If the space has directions written on it, follow the directions.

Have the players continue moving around the board and building castles until everyone reaches "Finish." Count up the number of castles each clan has built.

Golf

The game of golf originated in Scotland. With all of the green grassland available there, it is no wonder that golf is one of Scotland's favorite sports. Use a small, plastic miniature golf set in the classroom for this fun golfing activity. Set up the golf course by placing the cups or "holes" around the playing area. Place a numbered flag by each cup. On 3" x 5" (8 cm x 13 cm) index cards, write different commands, such as "Jump up and down 10 times" or "Count backwards from 100 by 5s." Place all of the cards in a small paper bag.

Have the children play golf as clans, letting one clan member golf each hole. Once a player has gotten the ball into the cup, have him select a card from the bag. The player reads the card aloud, and then everyone does the activity together. Continue golfing and drawing activities until everyone has reached the ninth hole.

Burns Night

Robert Burns is considered Scotland's national poet. On the anniversary of his birth on January 25, Scotland honors Burns with a celebration of dancing, bagpipes, and haggis. Haggis is a dish made from the insides of a cow and oatmeal that is then cooked in a casing made from the stomach of a sheep. The haggis is brought to the party, preceded by a bagpipe player, while someone reads Burns's "Ode to a Haggis" (a poem about haggis). While you may not be willing to try haggis, you can put your creative juices to work and cook up some Burns-like poetry.

Enlarge the Castle Game piece pattern at the top of this page so that it fills an entire page. Use correction fluid or a bit of white paper and tape to cover up the gate and create a large space for writing. Then make a copy of the castle for each child. Have the children practice writing poems or rhyming words on the castle entryway.

Highland Games

Another popular event in Scotland is the Highland Games. In the Highland Games, contestants compete with one another in feats of strength. Divide the class into clans, don your kilts, and head outside to compete in the following Highland favorites:

- Tossing the caber — In this activity, the contestant picks up a large pole. Holding it vertically in his hands, he flips the pole as far as he can. Find a long stick and simulate the caber-tossing activity. Use a measuring tape to measure each toss. Keep a running total to see how far the class can toss the caber together.

- Throwing the hammer — The hammer throw is a game in which an iron ball is attached to a bamboo stick. The contestant spins in place, swinging the ball around by the stick, then releases the stick to throw it. Stuff a tennis ball in the toe of a nylon stocking. Mark a circle on the playing field—this is where the children will try to throw the hammer. Have each contestant swing around once and then release the ball. Measure the distance thrown in steps and add to the previous tally.

- Putting the shot — The final activity is called the shot put. In this activity the contestant stands with his back toward the field. A heavy cannon ball is held on the shoulder close to the chin. The contestant then skips backwards, turns, and flings the ball. Use a large basketball for this activity. Have the children help you count how many times the ball bounces when it lands. Measure the distance of the throw from the circle to the spot where the ball landed. Tally up all of the throws for the class in this activity. Then add up all of the throws for the day to come up with a total distance the class tossed.

Loch Ness Diving

Loch Ness is a very deep, very beautiful, and very famous lake in Scotland. It gets its fame not from its beauty, but from what is said to lurk well beneath its surface. Loch Ness is the home of the fabled Loch Ness monster.

The Loch Ness monster, according to self-proclaimed eyewitnesses, is a large serpent-like sea creature that inhabits the lake. Although many people claim to have seen the Loch Ness monster, no one (scientist or otherwise) has yet been able to prove its existence. Share a book with the children that presents more thoughts and theories about the Loch Ness monster, such as *Loch Ness Monster* by Harriette Abels (Crestwood House, 1987). Be sure to reassure the children that the monster cannot hurt them.

Fill a large, deep bucket with water. In a separate bucket, place items that float and sink. Encourage the children to guess whether each item will sink or float like the Loch Ness monster once placed in the water. Have them test their theories by placing each item into the water, one at a time. Extend the activity to see if the children can make things that float sink or things that sink float. This might be accomplished by attaching one or more floating objects to one or more sinking objects. Provide tape, rubber bands, twist ties, paper clips, and other helpful materials for this part of the activity.

Sword Dancing

During celebrations, Scots often dance with swords. For a traditional sword dance, the dancer lays either two swords or one sword and a scabbard (a fancy sheath) across one another in the shape of an "X" and then dances around without stepping on the swords.

Make several X's on the floor with toy swords and scabbards or with masking tape. Play a selection of bagpipe music or sing the famous Scottish ballad "Loch Lomond" (see lyrics below). Put on your kilts and take turns dancing over the swords. If singing the "Loch Lomond" song, increase the tempo each time you sing the chorus so that the dancers have to go faster and faster.

Chorus from "Loch Lomond"

Oh! ye'll take the high road
And I'll take the low road,
And I'll be in Scotland afore ye;
For me and my true love

Will never meet again,
On the bonnie, bonnie banks
Of Loch Lomond.

Bruce and the Spider

Robert the Bruce was the king of Scotland hundreds of years ago. His army went to battle with England six times to fight for the freedom of Scotland. But during the sixth battle, his armies were scattered and Robert the Bruce was left alone. He hid in caves and thickets to avoid being captured by the English soldiers. One night while sitting in the cave, he spied a spider spinning a web. The spider was having difficulty. Six times the spider swung down trying to attach the web to the wall of the cave, and six times the spider failed. Robert the Bruce knew just how that spider felt. The spider climbed to the top of the web one more time, swung down and was finally successful at attaching the strand. If the spider could try again and succeed, then why couldn't Scotland? Robert the Bruce was inspired and went home immediately to rally the citizens of Scotland. They stood up to the advancing armies once more, and this time they succeeded in gaining freedom for Scotland.

It often takes courage and perseverance in order to succeed. Talk about times when the children had to work hard for something and finally achieved success after failing a few times. Have them write about and illustrate their experiences. Make little spiders out of black pom-poms and small sections of black chenille stems. Glue a spider to the top corner of each story to remind the children of Robert the Bruce and the spider.

Scottish Shortbread

Shortbread cookies are traditional Scottish sweets. Have the children help you make some with this simple recipe adapted from *Betty Crocker's Cookie Book* (New York: Golden Press, 1963):

3/4 c. (180 mL) butter or margarine
1/4 c. (60 mL) sugar
2 c. (470 mL) flour

Cream the butter and sugar. Mix in the flour. Chill the dough for 1 hour. Roll out the chilled dough to 1/2" (13 mm) thick and cut with a round cookie cutter about 2 1/2" (6 cm) in diameter. Use small cookie cutters to make impressions in the dough. Bake on an ungreased cookie sheet for 15 minutes at 350° F. Makes 4 1/2 dozen cookies.

Scottish Fairy Tales

Read some Scottish fairy tales, such as *Whuppity Stoorie* by Carolyn White (Putnam, 1997) or *The Black Bull of Norroway: A Scottish Tale*, retold by Charlotte Huck (Greenwillow, 2001). Have the children create costumes and act out the characters from the books as you or another child narrates the production.

Castle Game Board

Castle Game Board

Children in Traditional Scottish Dress

Flag of Scotland

Directions: Color the "X" white and the background blue.

Scottish Postcard, Globe Marker,
Luggage Sticker, and Passport Stamp

Postcard

Passport Stamp

Globe Marker

Luggage Sticker

South Africa

Capitals: Pretoria, Bloemfontein, and Cape Town
Official Languages: Afrikaans and 10 other languages

Officially known as the Republic of South Africa, the country of South Africa is located on the southern tip of the African continent. South Africa has three separate capitals: Pretoria (administrative), Bloemfontein (judicial), and Cape Town (legislative). There are 11 official languages in South Africa, but Afrikaans is recognized as the primary language.

Many years ago while trying to reach India, Dutchmen sailing around the cape discovered the native Bushmen. Soon many European settlers were putting down roots in South Africa. Here are some words and phrases in Afrikaans and Zulu to help you get started on your journey:

English	Afrikaans
Hello	Hallo
Good-bye	Tot siens
Thank you	Dankie
Please	Asseblief
Yes	Ja
No	Nee
1 – one	een
2 – two	twee
3 – three	drie
4 – four	vier
5 – five	vyf
6 – six	ses
7 – seven	sewe
8 – eight	agt
9 – nine	nege
10 – ten	tien

English	Zulu
Hello	Sawubona
How are you?	Unjani?
Good-bye	Hamba kahle (to person who is leaving)
Good-bye	Sala kahle (to person who is staying)
Please / Excuse me	Uxolo
Thank you	Ngiyabonga

For more information about South Africa:

Embassy of the Republic of South Africa
3051 Massachusetts Avenue NW
Washington, DC 20008
E-mail: info@saembassy.org

Phone: (202) 232-4400
Fax: (202) 265-1607
http://www.saembassy.org/

City of Gold

Johannesburg is a city that was built on gold—both literally and figuratively. Gold was discovered there in the earth, and as people began to mine it, the wealth from the gold produced the money to build, and so Johannesburg grew into a thriving, bustling city. Many people in South Africa today are employed by one of the country's many gold and platinum mines.

Purchase small, plastic gold coins and number them using a permanent marker. Make a poster showing a series of numbered circles that correspond to the numbers on the coins. Hide the coins throughout the classroom. As you visit and study South Africa, ask the children to watch for the gold coins. As they find them, attach the coins to the poster over the matching numbers. Once all of the coins have been found, the children can divide the coins on the poster evenly amongst themselves, then decide whether to keep them or trade them in for stickers or other small tokens.

Rainbow Nation

For many years, not all of the people of South Africa had a voice in their own government. The practice of apartheid, or segregation, was officially abolished in 1991. Now everyone, regardless of race, can vote for their country's leaders. South Africa adopted the name "Rainbow Nation" because it welcomed the freedom of all people in South Africa. Many of the national holidays celebrate this new policy and the people who fought to bring it about.

Make several copies of the South African Children in Traditional Dress pattern **(page 149)**. Have the children color as many kids as desired. Encourage them to color the skin and hair of each child differently from the others. On a 12" x 18" (30 cm x 46 cm) sheet of construction paper, have the children write, "South Africa is a rainbow nation." Glue the colored patterns onto the paper, and have the children add a sentence explaining why they feel it is important for people to have freedoms.

Bringing the Rain

Many people who live on the plains in South Africa live off of what they can grow on their farms. These self-supporting people do not have local grocery stores to go to when they need bread or fruit. They must make their own bread from the grains they grow on their land, harvest the fruits and vegetables from their gardens, and get meat, eggs, and milk from their own livestock. These people are particularly dependent on rain to bring much-needed water to their crops and animals. If too many seasons of drought go by, plants and animals will die, creating great hardship for the people. Many people believe that their actions (good or bad) can affect the weather. Read *Bringing the Rain to Kapiti Plain*, by Verna Aardema (New York: Dial Press, 1981). Talk about how Ki-pat solved his no-rain problem, and then have the children brainstorm other ways to "bring the rain."

African Safari

Africa is home to many animals. The "big five"—lions, rhinos, water buffalo, leopards, and elephants—are probably the most famous. Years ago, an African safari would have provided the opportunity to hunt these animals. But after years of misuse and hunting several animals to near extinction, South Africa now protects its herds and animals much more closely. Today, an African safari will take you into the game preserves where you can shoot pictures—not bullets—to capture these beautiful animals.

Make safari cameras with empty juice boxes. Tape the openings of empty juice boxes shut. Paint the boxes black or cover them with black paper. Make a copy of the Safari Camera and Photo pattern **(page 147)** for each child. Have the children color and cut out their camera patterns and glue them to the fronts of their juice boxes. Tape a 24" (61 cm) length of string to the sides of each camera so that it can be worn around the neck.

Collect pictures or replicas of African animals and place them around the classroom. Make a script for a guided tour that describes each animal and reveals a few interesting facts about the animal. Hold up a picture as you talk about each animal. Then hide the animals around the room. Have the children use their Safari binoculars (see Safari Binoculars activity below) to look at the animals as they find them on their safari. Have them take snapshots with their cameras of each animal they see. Make several copies of the photo frame pattern **(page 147)**. Make safari photo journals by folding several sheets of 9" x 12" (23 cm x 30 cm) construction paper in half. Staple several sheets together to make each child's book. After taking snapshots on the safari, have the children "develop" the pictures they have taken by drawing pictures of the animals in the photo frames. Glue these pictures inside the safari photo journals. Be sure to have the children document each photo by labeling it on the journal page and adding any important information about the animal.

Safari Binoculars

Make a copy of the Safari Binoculars pattern **(page 148)** on heavy card stock. Have the children color the binoculars as desired and cut them out along the solid border. Cut along the dotted lines where indicated inside the eyeholes. Fold these tabs in toward the back side of the binoculars. Staple two toilet tissue tubes together. Lay the binoculars facedown on the table and press down the tabs on the eyeholes. Set the toilet tissue tubes inside the eyeholes and tape or glue the tabs to the sides of the cardboard tubes. Punch two holes in the opposite end of the toilet tissue tubes and tie a length of yarn through the holes. The children can hang the binoculars around their necks and use them to help spot the wildlife on your African safari.

Zulus

The Zulus are one of the indigenous tribes of South Africa. The name Zulu means "people of Heaven," although many of the early Dutch explorers who fought fierce battles with the Zulus might disagree. The Zulus successfully fought off the invasion of European settlers and remain on their lands today. Zulus are actually quite friendly and hospitable. They are very loyal to their Inkosi, or leader of the tribe, who is regarded as a father figure. Zulus paint their bodies and dance, sing, and tell stories around bonfires. These ceremonies prepare the Zulus for battles, hunting, marriages, and other important events in the tribe.

There are many Zulu cave and rock paintings that date back thousands of years. These paintings tell stories of the Zulu tribes' everyday lives. They often depict scenes of hunting and the animals they interacted with on a daily basis.

Cut a large mountain shape out of brown craft paper. Crinkle it slightly to give it a three-dimensional appearance. Have the children use markers or chalk to draw their own rock paintings. Encourage them to draw pictures that depict their everyday lives and interests.

Beading

Beading is an important Zulu ritual. In fact, many Zulus use beads to express thoughts or feelings. Based on how she is feeling, a woman making a beaded bracelet might use a particular pattern to mean good luck or to express sorrow or revenge.

Provide the children with an assortment of beads. Choose natural colored beads of brown, yellow, white, taupe, etc. Provide the following key (adding to it as you wish) for the children to use when creating their beading patterns. When their bracelets are done, have the children trade with friends and see if their partners can discover what messages that they are sending with the beads:

Message	Pattern
I am happy today.	ABAB
I am your friend.	AABBCC
I am sad today.	ABBA
Let's play together.	AABCC
Have a good day.	ABBCBB

Sangoma

A *sangoma* is a traditional South African healer and fortune-teller. A sangoma uses shells, bones, and herbs to foretell a person's future. Gather a small assortment of sticks (for bones), shells, and herb stems and place them in a box. Wrap a turban around your head and have the children visit you one at a time to have their fortunes told. Shake up the contents of the box and spill it onto the table. Say something like "Oh my! This is a good fortune!" and proceed to add a fortune that tells of health, wealth, and any other good wishes you might have for each child. Have the children write their fortunes in their journals and tell how they feel about the fortunes they have been given.

Kalahari Desert

The Kalahari Desert covers a large area that encompases several African countries, including South Africa. The name means "the great thirst." Although most of the desert is made up of reddish-brown sand, other areas do receive a fair amount of rain and support the growth of some vegetation. Since the desert receives water only through precipitation, large cracks appear in the ground between the infrequent rains.

Using masking tape, tape a network of "cracks" on the floor in your classroom. Start in one area and radiate across to the other side of the room. Have the children walk on the cracks, following them from one side of the room to the other. Encourage them to walk in a variety of ways, including forwards, backwards, sideways, on tiptoe, and heel-to-toe. See how many times they can cross the Kalahari without falling off of the cracks. As a variation, see how quickly the children can move from one side of the room to the other without stepping on any cracks.

Crocodiles and Hippos

There are two major rivers in South Africa: the Orange and the Limpopo. Neither river is large enough to be a source of major travel or commerce, but both are inhabited by crocodiles and hippos. Hippos generally keep to themselves. Crocodiles, on the other hand, will attack if you get too close. The trouble is, both animals generally spend most of their time immersed in the river, so you do not know they are there until you are right next to them!

Create a river through your classroom by putting sheets of blue craft paper on the floor and marking off the banks of the river with masking tape. Write the words "hippo" and "crocodile" on enough 3" x 5" (8 cm x 13 cm) cards to have one card for each child. Choose three children to be "It." Have the rest of the children each choose a card, and instruct them not to tell anyone which cards they picked. Have the children with cards lie down on their backs on the floor "in the river." The players who are "It" now try to cross the river by stepping over the hippos and crocodiles. The trick is that they will not know which of the children are crocodiles and which are hippos until they step over them. Have one child attempt to cross at a time. If the child steps over a hippo, the hippo lies silently and lets him pass. If the child steps over a crocodile, the crocodile can grab his leg, and the child must return to the starting bank. Give each child three chances to cross the river without getting caught.

African Drums

Drums are an important part of traditional African culture. A typical African drum is made from a hollow tree and is decorated with beautiful patterns of lines, dots, and shapes. Collect a large empty can for each child. Have the child paint the sides of the drum and add a repeating pattern with paint or markers. Once the drums are ready, have the children sit in a circle with their drums in front of them. Use the drums to play a rhythm-matching game in which each child plays a rhythm that the other children try to repeat. Take turns around the circle so that everyone has a chance to lead the rhythm.

Batik

Though the technique originated in Indonesia, batik is a popular African handicraft of decorating cloth. It is usually done by taking a piece of cloth and drawing on it with wax. Dyes are then poured over the cloth and the dye adheres everywhere but where the wax was used. You can create a similar technique on paper. Use a white crayon to draw a picture or pattern on a sheet of construction paper. Pour thinned yellow, brown, orange, and black paint into shallow pans. Use a cotton ball to dip into the paint and paint over the wax images. The paint covers the paper everywhere except where the wax is used.

Safari Camera and Photo

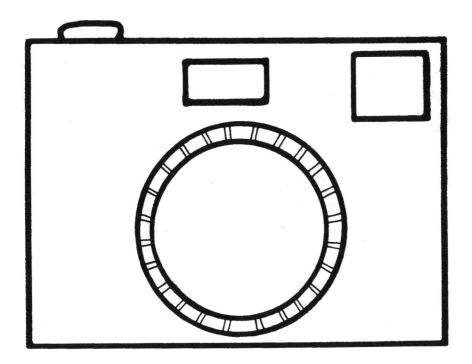

Safari Binoculars

TAB   TAB

Children in Traditional South African Dress

Flag of South Africa

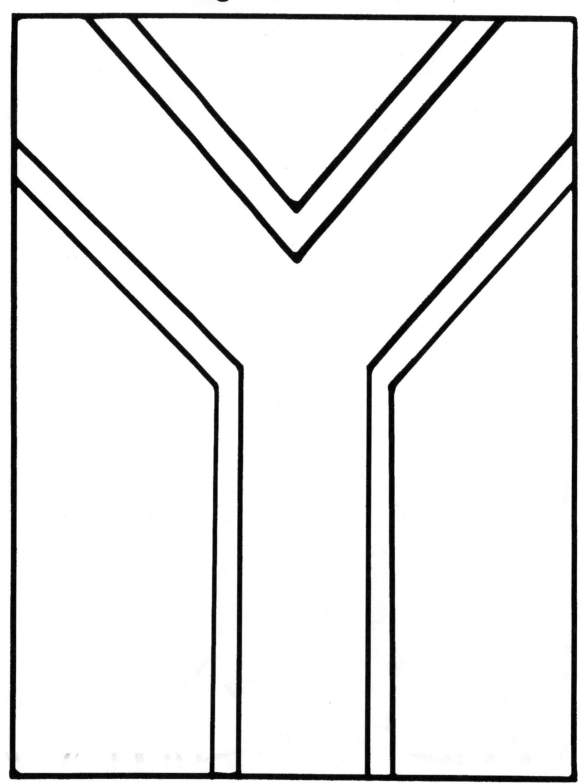

Directions: Color the horizontal "Y" green. Make the stripe above it red with a white border. The stripe below the "Y" is blue with a white border. Make the triangle black with a yellow border.

South African Postcard, Globe Marker, Luggage Sticker, and Passport Stamp

Postcard

Globe Marker

Passport Stamp

Luggage Sticker

Tahiti

Capital: Papeete
Official Languages: French and Tahitian

Tahiti is part of the French Polynesian islands in the middle of the Pacific Ocean. It is literally thousands of miles from any continent. Although there is some disagreement about which people first inhabited the islands, the Taata Maohi (tah-AH-ta mah-OH-hee), as the Tahitians call themselves, are proud of their culture and hope you will enjoy your visit to their island.

Prepare for a tropical adventure! Here are some words and phrases in French and Tahitian to help you get started:

English	French	Tahitian
Hello	*Bonjour*	*Ia orana*
Good-bye	*Au revoir*	*Parahi ia*
Yes	*Oui*	*E*
No	*Non*	*Aita*
Thank you	*Merci*	*Mauruuru*
You're welcome	*De rien*	*Aita e peapea*
1 – one	*un*	*ho'e*
2 – two	*deux*	*piti*
3 – three	*trois*	*toru*
4 – four	*quatre*	*maha*
5 – five	*cinq*	*pae*
6 – six	*six*	*ono*
7 – seven	*sept*	*hitu*
8 – eight	*huit*	*va'u*
9 – nine	*neuf*	*iva*
10 – ten	*dix*	*'ahuru*

Source: http://lc.byuh.edu/tahitian/lesson/framepract.html

For more information about Tahiti:

Embassy of France
4101 Reservoir Road NW
Washington, DC 20007
E-mail: info@amb-wash.fr

Phone: (202) 944-6000
Fax: (202) 944-6166
http://www.info-france-usa.org/

Polynesian Mythology

A myth is a story or a legend that attempts to explain events in nature. Tahitian mythology is filled with some very colorful creatures. One legend tells of how the people of Tahiti came into existence. Lake Vaihiria, which lies at the top of a mountain, is home to many eels. It is said that one of those eels crawled out of the lake one day and traveled down to the northern coast. There he married a beautiful maiden, and that was the beginning of the Tahitian people.

Other myths tell stories of gods. Maui is one of the more famous gods in Polynesian mythology. He was full of tricks and hijinks. He is credited with stories of lassoing the sun with a strand of his sister's hair in order to slow it down. Maui according to legend, lifted up the sky so that man could walk upright beneath it. Another tale tells of him fishing with his brothers. Maui's hook caught some land under the sea, and he told his brothers that it was a great fish. The brothers began rowing so earnestly that they did not notice the islands coming up out of the waters behind them. This is how Hawaii is said to have been created.

Share other stories of Polynesian mythology with the class. Then have the children write their own tales to explain natural events such as earthquakes, volcanoes, rain, sunsets, or snow.

Fruit Basket

Tahiti is home to many different kinds of fruit: guava, mango, banana, lime, grapefruit, orange, pineapple, cherimoya, and papaya, to name just a few. The Tahitians are very proud of their fruits, and only native Polynesians are allowed to sell them at the market in Papeete. (People of other cultures can only sell other goods.) Try to bring in one example of each fruit listed above. Have the children study the outside skins of the fruits, taking note of the different textures, sizes, and colors. Next, cut open the fruits to reveal the flesh inside. Again, have the children note the different colors and textures. Compare the seeds and consider whether the size of the seed is proportional to the size of the fruit. Count how many seeds are inside each fruit.

Cut the fruits into bite-sized pieces. Place each fruit in a separate bowl and label each bowl with a different letter of the alphabet. Make one card one for each child with those same letters in a random order, such as HDGAFICBE. Give the children each a wooden skewer and a card, and have them make fruit kebabs following the order listed on their cards. Vary the activity by using the labeled bowls and cards for patterning activities. Enjoy the fruit for a snack.

To play the fruit basket game, have all of the children sit in chairs in a circle. You will need one less chair than you have children. Give each child the name of a fruit. (Stick with three or four familiar fruits for younger children.) One child is "It" and stands in the middle of the circle. She calls out the name of a fruit, and all of the children with that fruit name get up and exchange seats as quickly as possible. The child who is "It" tries to take one of their seats. The child left without a chair is "It" for the next round. If desired, the child who is "It" can call out two fruits at a time or call "Fruit basket!" in which case everyone gets up to exchange seats at the same time.

Arii

The *arii* (ah-REE-ee) is the chief of a Polynesian tribe. In the past, it was customary for the chief to always be higher than his subjects. Therefore, the chief was carried on the shoulders of his people wherever he went. If he stood, the subjects had to sit. If he sat, the subjects had to lay down on the floor.

Play this fun Chief Arii stretching activity. Tell the class that you are the arii, or chief. Your subjects (i.e., the children) must always be lower than you are. If you stoop, they must stoop lower. If you sit, they must lay on the ground. Stand in front of the class and alternately stand, stoop, and sit while the children hustle to get lower than you. Swap places with your best subject and play again.

Coconut Groves

Tahiti has many coconut groves. The coconuts are relatively soft when picked, and the tops can be hacked off with a machete to drink the milk inside. Once harvested, the coconuts are laid out in the sun to dry. Purchase a fresh coconut and let the children examine it. Using a hammer and nail, pound holes in the eyes of the coconut. Pour the coconut milk into a cup, and let the children smell it and swirl it around. Ask them how it compares to cow's milk or fruit juice. Wrap the drained coconut in two plastic bags and continue to hammer it until it breaks open. Take the coconut pieces out of the bag and carefully use a sharp knife to dig out the coconut flesh. Share the coconut with the children, and talk about how we are accustomed to eating fruits and foods that are common to where we live. Children in Tahiti eat coconuts and drink coconut milk frequently, but this may be a first for most of the children in your class. Ask the children to imagine a fruit or vegetable that is grown locally that the children in Tahiti might find fascinating.

Beaches

Some of the beaches in Tahiti are covered in black sand. This is due to the volcanic deposits and erosion that occurred long, long ago when the island was first created. Another interesting fact about Tahiti is that there are no plants with thorns growing there. You can walk through the forests, mountains, and beaches barefooted and never encounter a painful thorn.

One thing that you must watch out for, however, is sea urchins. These spiny ocean creatures sting when touched. Draw several simple sea urchins on the backs of paper plates (or on sheets of paper) by drawing circles covered with spines. Take another stack of paper plates (or sheets of paper) and make a beach grid on the floor that is 10 plates wide and 10 plates high. Place the sea urchins randomly throughout the grid (see example). Have the children work in teams of two or three. Have one partner roll a die. The other partners must start at one end of the beach grid and move the number of spaces indicated on the die. The trick is to take steps while navigating around the sea urchins. The first person across the beach rolls the die for the next beach walk.

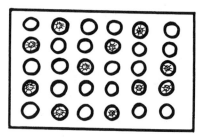

Fishing Huts

Tahitian fishermen build small bamboo huts to house their fishing gear and for shelter while they are preparing to fish. These round huts are made with walls of bamboo and roofs of banana or palm leaves. Make a series of fishing huts for quiet reading time during your travels to Tahiti.

To make the walls of each hut, cut an opening in a large appliance box. Have the children roll newspaper or craft paper to create bamboo poles and glue these onto the sides of the box. Cut large palm leaves out of green craft paper and attach these to the top for the roof of the hut. Encourage the children to go inside the huts for some quiet thinking time or to read books.

Heiva i Tahiti

One of the biggest celebrations in Tahiti lasts nearly a month—from the end of June through July, peaking on July 14, Bastille Day. Heiva i Tahiti is filled with feasts and events. There are song-and-dance competitions, canoe races, javelin-throwing contests, and footraces. Arts and crafts and cooking demonstrations are also popular, where you can learn about different ways to prepare coconut and how to weave with leaves. One of the more unusual events in the celebration is the fruit-bearer's race. In this event, large quantities of fruit are tied to opposite ends of long sticks. The racers then dash to the finish line while carrying the sticks loaded with fruit over their shoulders.

Plan your own Heiva i Tahiti celebration with some of the following activities:

- Have the children divide into small groups and plan song-and-dance numbers to perform in front of the class.

- Use drinking straws as javelins and toss them across the room from a marked point. Use a tape measure to see how far each javelin is thrown.

- Take two broom handles and tie plastic shopping bags filled with blocks on either end of both handles. Divide the class into two teams and hold a fruit-bearer's race.

- Tahitian *more* (mo-RAY) skirts look like grass skirts, but they are actually made from the bark of hibiscus trees. Make your own more skirts out of layers of newspaper cut into thin strips. Attach the strips together at one end with a wide strip of masking tape. Make ties out of strips of folded tape and staple to the ends of the skirts. Boys wear knee-length skirts and girls wear ankle-length skirts. Add tassles and flowers to adorn the waist.

- Create shell necklaces. Make several copies of the Shell Necklace pattern **(page 155)** on heavy card stock. Have the children color and cut out the shells. Punch two holes in each shell where indicated by small "X's," and lace them onto a 24" (61 cm) length of string. Have the children create a variety of patterned necklaces with the shells.

- Fold several sheets of tissue paper in half. Gather the sheets around the middle and tie with a twist tie. Gently peel back the layers of paper to make a flower. Tuck the flower behind an ear, or make several flowers and twist them into a floral wreath for the head.

- Make horizontal slits about 1" (25 mm) apart in several sheets of 12" x 20" (30 cm x 51 cm) green construction paper. Then cut several 2" (5 cm) strips of construction paper. Have the children fold the strips in half lengthwise and weave them through the slits in the large sheet of green paper. Use the finished mats for serving fruit or tapioca pudding. (Tapioca comes from the root of the manioc tree, which is found in Tahiti.)

Black Pearls

Black pearls are an exotic treasure produced by the black-lipped mother-of-pearl oyster. A special dark pigment secreted by the mollusk makes the pearls dark in color. It takes two years to create just one pearl. Black pearls used to be so rare that only royalty could wear them. Now they are cultured (produced with the help of people), and while still exotic, anyone willing to pay the price may have one. Make your own black pearl jewelry by threading round black beads onto 2" (5 cm) chenille stems. Twist the ends of each stem together to make a ring. Use the rings as incentives for good behavior.

Seashell Necklaces

Children in Traditional Tahitian Dress

Flag of Tahiti

Directions: Color the stripes of the flag: red, white, and red (top to bottom).

Tahitian Postcard, Globe Marker,
Luggage Sticker, and Passport Stamp

Postcard

Globe Marker

Luggage Sticker

Passport Stamp

Bibliography

- Allison, Robert J. *Australia*. Austin, TX: Raintree Steck-Vaughn, 1996.

- Arora Lal, Sunandini. *India*. Countries of the World Series. Milwaukee, WI: Gareth Stevens, 1999.

- Baines, John. *Japan*. Austin, TX: Raintree Steck-Vaughn, 1994.

- Binns, Tony, and Rob Bowden. *South Africa*. The Changing Face of Series. Austin, TX: Raintree Steck-Vaughn, 2002.

- Borlenghi, Patricia, and Rachel Wright. *Italy*. New York: Franklin Watts, 1993.

- Cumming, David. *India*. Country Insights Series. Austin, TX: Raintree Steck-Vaughn, 1998.

- Goh Sui Noi. *China*. Countries of the World Series. Milwaukee, WI: Gareth Stevens, 1998.

- Greenblatt, Miriam. *Iran*. New York: Children's Press, 2003.

- Ilyin, Andrey. *A Child's Day in a Russian City*. New York: Benchmark Books, 2001.

- Morris, Ting and Neil, and Rachel Wright. *Germany*. New York: Franklin Watts, 1993.

- NgCheong-Lum, Roseline. *Tahiti*. Cultures of the World Series. New York: Benchmark Books, 1997.

- O'Sullivan, MaryCate. *Scotland*. Faces and Places Series. Chanhassen, MN: Child's World, 2002.

- Phillips, Charles, editor. *Brazil*. Grolier Educational, 1997.

- Schemenauer, Elma. *Iran*. Faces and Places Series. Chanhassen, MN: Child's World, 2001.

- Serra, Mariana. *Brazil*. Food and Festivals Series. Austin, TX: Raintree Steck-Vaughn, 2000.

- Shalant, Phyllis. *Look What We've Brought You from India: Crafts, Games, Recipes, Stories, and Other Cultural Activities from Indian Americans.* Parsippany, NJ: Julian Messner, 1998.

- Sheehan, Sean, and Angela Black. *Jamaica*. Cultures of the World Series. New York: Benchmark Books, 1996.

- Stein, R. Conrad. *Mexico*. Enchantment of the World Series. New York: Children's Press, 1998.